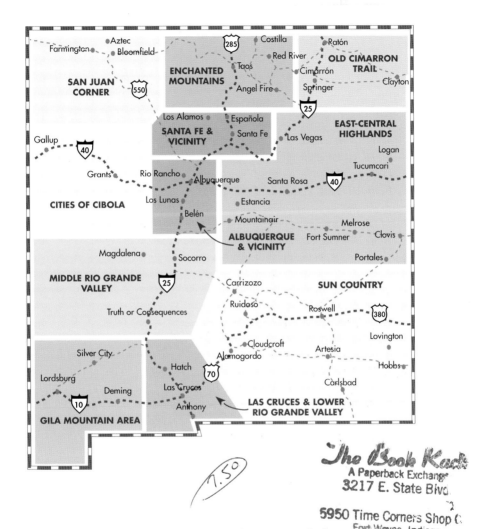

Front cover—*Angie Gurulé-Vergo and Jim Vergo of Albuquerque spend time with their dog Buddy in the aspen-covered forest of the Sangre de Cristo Mountains northeast of Santa Fe. Angie retired after working more than 30 years at Sandia National Laboratories and Jim moved to New Mexico after a 30-year career with a gas company in Chicago. Photo by LeRoy N. Sanchez.*

Author: James Burbank

Editor: Arnold Vigil

Book Design and Production: Bette Brodsky

Publisher: Ethel Hess

Library of Congress Catalog Card Number:
2001-135826
ISBN: 0-937206-74-1

Second Printing, October 2005

NEW MEXICO
M A G A Z I N E

RETIREMENT NEW MEXICO

3RD EDITION REVISED & UPDATED

A COMPLETE

GUIDE

TO

RETIRING

IN

NEW

MEXICO

BY JAMES BURBANK

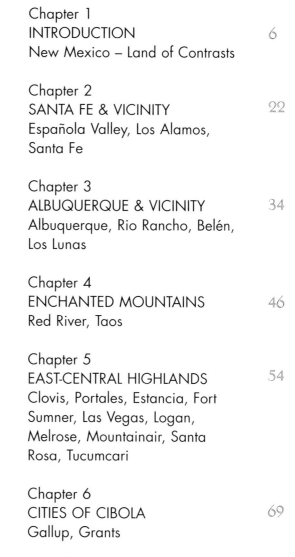

TABLE OF
CONTENTS

Welcome to the third edition of *Retirement New Mexico!* Much has changed since the last revision was completed in 1996. Since then the Internet and e-mail have revolutionized communications. Today, most of New Mexico's chambers of commerce have new Web sites and you can communicate with them directly through e-mail. Originally, and for subsequent editions of this book, some chambers provided us much useful information for this indispensable guide to the state's retirement resources. Of course, this invaluable contact information is provided to facilitate your ability to learn as much as possible about our enchanting state's retirement resources.

Over the years many retirees have written me about the book. Your letters mean a lot to me, and I've had fun corresponding with you directly and getting to know you personally. I've taken great pains to contact experts in the retirement towns we feature to ensure we have concise retirement information about New Mexico. Of course, sometimes changes occur, especially in regard to cost-of-living information, housing and retirement facilities in our communities. We've tried to keep you abreast of the latest trends in our communities to provide you the most useful guide possible to all that New Mexico offers retirees. After you read the book, I highly advise contacting chambers of commerce through e-mail in the towns you are interested in for the latest

Above—*Aromatic chamisa bushes in full bloom paint the landscape in front of the majestic Sangre de Cristo Mountains in the Taos area of northern New Mexico. Photo by Mark Nohl,* New Mexico Magazine.

information about relocating in a particular community. They can refer you to local experts to help you in your search.

So, what's it like retiring in New Mexico? The best way of finding out comes directly from the horse's mouth. Here's what two former Midwest retirees experienced when they decided to move to New Mexico:

Another New Mexico winter morning began for former Illinois residents Bill Thomas and his wife, Mary. Bill looked out over his patio in Albuquerque's Northeast Heights and saw the towering Sandía Mountains etched in stark contrast against the brilliant, blue New Mexico sky. Piñon smoke wafted through the dry, crisp air. Bill chopped a small log to add to the fire he was building before breakfast. He thought about his careful efforts to plan his retirement, efforts that he felt were now paying off.

When Bill reached 62, he began to consider places where he thought life might be more fulfilling than in the Chicago area where he worked as a trust officer for a suburban bank. Bill and Mary were both tired of the hustle and bustle of their Midwest lifestyle, of humid, bone-chilling gray winters, and of fighting traffic. Bill consulted his doctor about possible retirement health issues, and he started to do extensive reading to learn about relocation prospects. Bill and Mary considered many alternatives in the three years before he retired. Finally, they decided to come to New Mexico.

"There were a heck of a lot of reasons why we chose New Mexico," Bill says.

Bill and Mary like the outdoors. Their love of the wide-open spaces was one of the major reasons they kept returning to New Mexico for vacations that had introduced them to the whole state, from its vast desert vistas to the wild northern mountains. They loved this land, its people and cultures. So when it came time for Bill to finally "hang up his spurs," they both agreed—New Mexico seemed to be the place for them. Before committing themselves to a final decision, however, they packed up their RV and headed out to give New Mexico living a try. They spent about six months in various parts of the state. Theirs was a hard decision because they loved so much about New Mexico. But the central region won out because it had the blend of urban services and wilderness accessibility they wanted. Albuquerque, with its medium-sized metropolitan atmosphere, convenient medical facilities and proximity to wilderness recreation, seemed perfect.

Mary's best friend, Marla Jones, and her husband, Thad, had also decided to come west from Chicago to New Mexico, but because of Marla's arthritis, they chose to locate in Las Cruces in the southern part of the state because of its mild winter temperatures in the mid-50s and precipitation of only 8 inches a year.

Independent sources give high marks to New Mexico towns and cities as retirement centers. Las Cruces, Roswell, Albuquerque, Deming and Santa Fe were rated by Rand McNally in 1988 as among the top-100 towns in the country for retirement.

Signet books chose Santa Fe as one of the 100 best cities in which to retire from a field of 18,000 municipalities, and it ranked New Mexico the sixth-best state in the country for retirement prospects. There are many reasons why New Mexico is an attractive American retirement location.

NEW MEXICO—HEALTHY CLIMATE, EASY LIFESTYLE

Many people who are planning to retire are surprised to learn that New Mexico has the lowest death rate from heart attacks of any state in the continental United States.

Doctors theorize that even mild exercise at higher elevations might actually account for people being in better shape than those who are in lower elevations. However, if you are considering a high-altitude retirement relocation, you should consult your doctor, especially if you have heart trouble or other problems that could be affected by elevation. Once adjusted, though, many seniors find high-altitude living vigorous and refreshing. And there are many places in New Mexico's lower elevations that have an ideal range of temperature and low humidity for pleasant, easy living.

The body functions best at about 66 degrees Fahrenheit with a relative humidity of 55 percent. Maximum efficiency without physical strain is the goal if you want to plan your retirement in a location that will promote your health. Ideally, the temperature-humidity index should be less than 72.

Physicians recommend the southern part of New Mexico for those who suffer from arthritis, rheumatism, emphysema, sinus and other respiratory problems, as well as hypertension and heart disease.

Warm weather and blue, open skies tend to make people feel better physically and psychologically. Changes in weather affect pulse rate, body temperature and metabolism. New Mexico is famous for its abundant sunshine (256 days a year) and turquoise skies.

Climatic conditions in New Mexico offer a rich variety of settings, scenery and weather to the prospective retiree. While 85 percent of New Mexico, the fifth largest state in the country, lies above 4,000 feet, elevations range from 2,850 feet in the Pecos River Basin near Carlsbad to 13,161 feet at Wheeler Peak far to the north near Taos.

The Continental Divide enters the state near Chama at the Colorado border and wanders south, leaving the state through Hidalgo County in the far southwest corner.

New Mexico's semiarid, subtropical climate features light precipitation, abundant sunshine and low relative humidity. Many people think of New Mexico as a desert with sand dunes and cactus. This image is far from the truth. The state offers one of the greatest varieties of ecological zones in the world.

In the north-central mountains, snowfall usually reaches 300 inches from December to March. To the south, in the lower Río Grande Valley, winter-to-spring snowfalls are only about 2 inches a year. In every part of New Mexico

Above—*Brilliant golden-yellow leaves on aspen trees in the Santa Fe National Forest delight many nature lovers in autumn but also signal the upcoming winter season. Photo by Mark Nohl,* New Mexico Magazine.

the sun shines more than 70 percent of the year. Mornings are cool with 60 percent humidity; afternoon humidity tapers to 30 percent.

In most parts of the state dramatic thunderstorms with giant cumulus clouds and impressive lightning displays during July and August bring much of the state's rainfall. At the highest elevation alpine tundra extends to spruce and fir forests at 8,000 to 12,000 feet. High mountains in the western two-thirds of the state are forested with firs, ponderosa pines and Arizona pines. Below 7,500 feet piñon and juniper trees extend over low hills, plateaus and mountains. In the southern quarter, oaks, sumacs and manzanitas give way to open plains and broad valleys covered with creosote bushes, mesquite and desert sage.

Mountains and mesas are interspersed by plains covered with grama grass and buffalo grass. These plains seem to extend forever toward open horizons dominated by wide blue sky counterpointed by dramatic clouds.

ENCHANTED TRAILS—A LAND WHERE HISTORY LIVES

This landscape still speaks to the imagination of early days in the great Southwest. History lives and rich cultural diversity contributes its own particular flavor to the New Mexico experience. More than 400 years ago the conquistadores entered this region so reminiscent of parts of their own native Spain. Here they discovered the sacred homeland of the Keresan, Tewa, Towa, Tiwa and other Pueblo tribes. Bordered by mountains and delineated by the Río Grande and the surrounding desert plains, the Pueblos lived a harmonious existence based on agriculture and traditions that were already ancient when the Spanish arrived. Since then the rich pageant of events that is New Mexico history has left an enduring legacy that remains evident today.

Around 1610, the year Galileo invented the telescope, construction had already begun on the Palace of the Governors in Santa Fe, which was founded by Gov. Pedro de Peralta as the capital of *Nuevo México* (New Mexico). In Alcala, Spain, during the same year, the epic poem *Historia de la Nueva México* was published and it described the colonization of New Mexico by Don Juan de Oñate. Oñate and his small band of 129 soldiers and 10 Franciscans completed his conquest in 1599 after laying siege to rebellious Acoma Pueblo.

An uneasy period of Spanish settlement followed until most of the settlers and Franciscans in outlying areas were forced out during the Pueblo Revolt of 1680. Resettlement quickly proceeded during the next decade, and New Mexico remained the northern frontier of the Viceroyalty of New Spain until the 1820s.

Irrigation ditches, called *acequias*, were established that still are a part of the state's agricultural life. Spanish governors issued land grants to individuals and to groups who set up separate communities and often held grazing land in common. This colonial way of life with its folkways, color and traditions continued through the Mexican Period from 1821 until 1846, which marked the beginning of the U.S. occupation.

Ten years before the Civil War, westward immigration, which had begun as a trickle with the opening of the Santa Fe Trail in 1821 and was fueled by the California gold strike, brought settlers to New Mexico. Oñate's dream of the Seven Cities of Cíbola seemed to resurrect from the desert earth, firing gold prospectors who swarmed west in search of riches. Secession of the South saw a brief period of Confederate occupancy in La Mesilla and Santa Fe. Two major battles were fought in the state. But the Union recaptured New Mexico and the war later came to an end.

Civil conflict was soon replaced by strife with Indian nations and growing influence of the ranching industry. Geronimo, Pancho Villa, Billy the Kid and Pat Garrett—these and other names contribute to the historical riches waiting to be discovered in this land. New Mexico's past is close enough to touch for those who choose to retire in the Land of Enchantment.

For the Western territories, a new spirit of unprecedented growth began with the building of the railroad in the 1880s. Yet New Mexico, in part because of its profound Hispanic and Indian traditions, continued to have its own cultural life separate from other Western areas, though it was influenced by a major influx from the East and Midwest. Not until 1912 did the territory finally become a state, following congressional passage of the Enabling Act signed by President William Howard Taft that called for a New Mexico constitutional convention in 1910. New Mexico still preserves its distinctive multicultural heritage, which today makes it such a unique and interesting place to discover.

WORLD OF SUN AND HARMONY—
CULTURAL TRADITIONS ABOUND

If you want to sample a world apart where traditions offer ancient ways of life filled with beauty, New Mexico is the place for you. Imagine walking the streets of Acoma, the oldest inhabited city in the country. The very same pueblo laid siege by Juan de Oñate in the late 1500s is perched on a mesa overlooking miles of high desert on all sides and is a short 60 miles west of Albuquerque. Picture yourself watching the celebration of Shalako at dusk when 10-foot-high, birdlike dancers in eagle and raven feathers and blue masks swoop adroitly through the Pueblo village of Zuni. They enter their ceremonial houses and begin a nightlong vigil that ends at dawn when final prayers are intoned and sacred corn meal is sprinkled on the dancers. Living in New Mexico lets you discover other cultures without leaving home.

Ritual animal dances of the Pueblo Indians vividly show the respect native peoples retain for the natural world. The intriguing *Tablita* and *Matachines* dances, with all their color, open a whole world of mystery and magical significance to the visitor.

For those who want to sample or collect arts and crafts created by masters, New Mexico provides examples of pottery making, weaving and painting to please and excite even the most fastidious collector.

Hispanic traditions and folkways are alive and well in New Mexico. From the Santuario de Chimayó to the many local fiestas, missions and *moradas* (*Penitente* chapels), New Mexico is unique in preserving expressions of a culture inherited from the earliest days of colonial settlement. New Mexico has a host of Hispanic customs that are found only in this region. New Mexico food offers its own special variations of Hispanic and Indian dishes.

OUTDOOR ADVENTURES NEW MEXICO STYLE

Since the sun shines just about every day in New Mexico, a wealth of outdoor activities awaits those who retire to this enchanted land. Every season features its own variety of fun. Summer months offer activities that can be year-round in some parts of the state: camping, hiking, horseback riding and fishing in state and national parks. Mountain climbing or river rafting invite the adventure of a lifetime. Swimming, golf and tennis facilities can readily be located through city recreation departments and chambers of commerce. Cyclists will find plenty of opportunities to bicycle on local side roads and designated bike trails.

During winter, 10 major ski areas in the state offer downhill enthusiasts a variety of trails for the novice to the expert. Cross-country skiing, snowshoeing, snowmobiling, ice fishing and skating are popular in some areas. New Mexico gives the hunter a variety of terrain and quarry.

New Mexico is a rockhound's paradise. Some 440 minerals can be collected here; only California claims more. There are a number of rockhounder clubs that can provide information on specific locations throughout the state. New Mexico has 45 state parks and preserves, five state monuments, two national parks and 10 national monuments. Many points of interest have picnicking, camping and hiking trails, while others offer scenic, historic or geologic interest. State monuments, managed by the Museum of New Mexico, preserve historic or archaeological sites.

Visiting ghost towns is also popular in the state, and there are more than a dozen sites that are interesting to poke around in for a taste of what remains of the 1880s heydays. The Pueblo, Apache and Navajo reservations draw visitors to observe public celebrations as well as to enjoy recreational opportunities.

New Mexico has an unusually rich artistic life. Georgia O'Keeffe was a longtime resident of northern New Mexico and the state left its indelible mark on her paintings. The visual arts are particularly feted in Santa Fe, where many galleries feature works by top Southwestern artists. The world-famous Santa Fe Opera presents a summer season of elegant entertainment under the stars.

New Mexico is also the haunt of many writers. The Taos writers' circle of the 1920s and '30s had many illustrious members. D.H. Lawrence's ranch near Taos is now the property of the University of New Mexico. Mabel Dodge Luhan and Spud Johnson were other colorful figures from this era. Today many writers and authors, intrigued by the romance of New Mexico, make the state their home.

NEW MEXICO RETIREMENT LIVING—A FEW NOTES

The Federal Older Americans Act requires that the New Mexico State Agency on Aging follow a plan for delivering services for the state's elderly. During the first three years of the new century (2000-2003) the agency will address developing trends in the state's senior population—trends you should be aware of when you are considering relocating here.

Between 1990 and 2025 the state anticipates the population of New Mexicans age 65 and older will increase by 170 percent. This increase includes a large percentage of minorities, most of whom (about a third) are Hispanic. These developments place a considerable burden on the state's senior resources for those who have insufficient financial resources or who have not planned for retirement. Since per capita health-care spending is 3.5 percent greater for those over the age of 65, these trends underscore the need for seniors to maintain a healthy and active lifestyle. The U.S. Department of Health and Human Services estimated that between 1990 and 2000 the number of people entering nursing homes in the state increased by 52 percent, while the projected national growth was estimated at 27 percent. This figure represents the fifth-fastest growth rate in the nation. Funding changes in Medicare caused by the Balanced Budget Act have cut monies for home-health care by 41 percent. As a result, since 1997, 70 home-health-care providers in New Mexico have gone out of business, leaving about 100 to provide home-health-care services in the state. Similar financial pressures are being experienced by other providers here as a result of these national trends. The fastest

Above—*Pueblo Indian dancers do their part to preserve centuries-old native culture. Many pueblos throughout New Mexico welcome visitors to their annual feast day celebrations. Photo by Chris Corrie.*

rate of population growth for seniors is among those who are 85 years and older. Increasing age means an increased potential for physical impairment and frailty. State facilities to provide for these people may be outstripped by these ever-growing needs, the State Agency on Aging fears. Obviously these rather sobering trends favor those who are financially prepared and who follow active healthy lifestyles, both factors that this book strongly advocates for readers.

Fortunately the State Agency on Aging, which is gearing up to meet these demands, provides a host of services for you if you are considering relocating to New Mexico. The state is a national innovator in developing services for retirees. The agency acts to provide benefits counseling for seniors, legal referrals and education, job training and employment counseling, senior-safety counseling, volunteer opportunities, support-service networking, caregiver support and longterm-care information and advocacy.

In 1985 New Mexico passed the Continuing Care Act to provide to prospective and actual residents information about the ownership, operation and finances of communities offering life-care arrangements. Many retirees who come to New Mexico wonder what kind of living arrangements the state offers. In the past many retirement communities charged residents entry fees or endowments in exchange for providing lifetime on-site medical care. Nationally and locally, substantial fees for such services and the financial failure of some communities have focused attention on such arrangements for retired living.

The agency advises, for instance, that if you sign a contract for continuing care, certain information must by law appear in your agreement. The State Agency on Aging and the Attorney General's office are both excellent sources of information on the act. The State Agency on Aging administers a variety of programs of interest to retirees and acts as an information clearinghouse and an advocate for the older population in the state.

Thorough investigation of any living arrangement involving fees for promised medical care, other services and/or rent is essential, and seeking the advice of a lawyer or financial advisor who is fully aware and knowledgeable about your intention to contract for continuing care is highly advisable. Basically there are two approaches for delivering services under a life-care or continuing-care arrangement.

The "insurance model" involves payment of a substantial entrance fee and monthly fees based on the type of residence and services provided, such as meals and transportation in addition to medical care should you need it. Monthly fees might increase but should not go up in the event you must transfer to a nursing-care facility.

A "fee-for-service" community does not always charge an entrance fee. If it does, the fee is usually less than that charged in the insurance-model community. Charges are assessed for each service used, with nursing-home care charged per day. Many such communities give residents a reduced charge for nursing care. In some cases a certain number of free days might be given to a resident needing nursing care.

Some communities use a combination approach, offering a service package for a monthly fee. You should be aware that any community that asks you to transfer all your assets to pay entrance deposits and monthly fees is violating the law. You cannot legally turn over all your assets to a community in return for personal care. Hard experience in the early days of life-care programs when total asset transfer was common has shown that placing residents in the hands of a provider, making them totally dependent, was a bad idea. If such communities failed, residents had no resources to start over.

The State Agency on Aging publishes a book that is an invaluable resource for learning more specifics about the act and how you can protect yourself: *Consumer's Guide to Continuing Care Communities*. It is available by writing the State Agency on Aging, 228 E. Palace Ave., Santa Fe, N.M. 87501; *(505) 827-7640, (800) 432-2080 (toll free in New Mexico). You can also contact the agency at 1410 San Pedro NE, Albuquerque, N.M.; *(505) 255-0971, (866) 842-9230 (toll free in New Mexico). I also highly recommend visiting the agency's website (www.nmaging.state.nm.us), a very detailed and specific tool that provides links to other senior resources here.

New Mexico does not have planned-retirement resort cities such as those in Florida, Arizona, California and a few other states. Most people prefer rental housing or they invest in their own private residences. The average selling price per square foot of living space in the New Mexico housing market ranks as one of the lowest in the nation.

New Mexico recorded a population of 1.3 million in the 1980 census. During the 2000 census the state recorded a population of 1,819,046. The state is still remarkably uncongested. Be prepared for the feel of wide-open spaces. The Albuquerque metro region, with a population of about 700,000, is the state's largest city. Each place, large or small, has its own ambiance.

Be sure to check out medical facilities in the area you are considering. While the state has good medical care in general, some communities lack in-depth services. Obviously, the towns where retirees congregate will be conscious of services needed by those who choose to locate there.

There are about 166 senior centers and meal sites in New Mexico. Each county has one or more active programs. Senior centers can be good sources of information on the basics. You will also want to check with the local chamber of commerce to become attuned to specifics in your area.

People often wonder what kind of employment opportunities are here for older people with professional and technical backgrounds. Jobs in these areas are available, but they are not plentiful. The Employment Security Office in each major town can provide you with some information about salaried positions for retired and older workers.

New residents need to apply for a New Mexico driver's license within 30 days. On surrendering your past license, you must pass an eye test and a

*See Page 21 for area code information.

Above—*The expansive vistas, abundant sunshine and generally pleasant climate make the state an ideal place to golf. Every corner of the state has plenty of choices to golf amidst beautiful terrain like this at Cochití Lake. Photo by Chris Corrie.*

written test. The four-year license requires a $16 fee.

If you are looking for educational opportunities, New Mexico has a university, community college and business-school system that is well-developed. Adult education courses are available in many public schools and through institutions of higher learning. Elderhostel programs, book-discussion clubs and many other informal educational opportunities can be found in many towns.

TAX CONSIDERATIONS

A major consideration for relocating to New Mexico is the state's tax system affecting retirees. Among the most equitable in the country, the state's tax structure for retirees competes favorably with other tax systems in the United States.

Property taxes are among the lowest in the U.S. New Mexico ranks 49th in the country on property-tax burden. All real and tangible property is assessed at 33.3 percent. Individuals with a modified gross income of up to $16,000 can receive a tax-credit rebate of up to $250.

Personal-income tax also is low for senior citizens in comparison with other states. Taxable income is based on federal adjusted-gross income with reductions for personal-exemption allowances, standard deductions and excess federal-itemized deductions.

Beginning at age 65, all taxpayers qualify for a state $8,000 exemption in addition to the federal exemption. The state exemption starts to level off as adjusted-gross income climbs above $30,000 for married taxpayers filing jointly (at $18,000 for single taxpayers).

Other tax laws of interest to retirees include the state's estate tax, gross-receipts tax and succession tax. The estate tax is a 10 percent credit against the federal tax and is imposed on the transfer of the net estate in an amount equal to the federal credit. The succession tax applies only to those estates where the deceased died before 1972 and there is land involved. It does not affect new retirees. A state gross-receipts tax of 5 percent is levied on all receipts of tangible property sold or leased and services sold. Local add-ons could figure up to as much as 2.8725 percent more.

There is no gift tax.

A WORD ABOUT TRANSPORTATION

How do you get around in New Mexico? Although by most comparisons the state is thinly populated, traveling around New Mexico or seeking inter-state transport is not difficult.

Two international airports serve the state. In the north-central region, the recently expanded Albuquerque International is one of the fastest growing airports in the country and offers national and international flights. El Paso International Airport across the border in Texas serves the southern part of the state. Both provide service for major carriers and charters. In-state flights are provided by Ross Aviation (between Albuquerque and Los Alamos) and by Mesa Airlines, serving Alamogordo, Albuquerque, Carlsbad, Clovis, Farmington, Gallup, Hobbs and Roswell. Most towns and cities have airports or landing strips and some have charter service.

Interstate bus service is provided by Greyhound, which travels through-out the state. The smaller Navajo Transit System gives a regional service out of Gallup, going as far as Flagstaff, Ariz. If you are interested in trains, AMTRAK direct service is provided to the following locations: Albuquerque, Deming, Lordsburg, Ratón, Las Vegas, Lamy (Santa Fe) and Gallup.

HOW TO USE THIS BOOK

We conducted a thorough investigation of retirement living in New

Mexico specifically designed to provide a single, authoritative informational source containing what you need to know when considering retirement in the Land of Enchantment. We conducted a detailed investigation of each community included in this book. Each city or town prepared a lengthy response to a specially designed questionnaire. We then conducted independent personal interviews with government representatives, members of the business community and retired residents in each location.

The beginning of each section lists key points about a particular locale, followed by a description of the area in general. Finally, each town or city is covered in detail. Historical information of interest and comments by retirees living in the location are also included, as well as noteworthy attractions within motoring distance of the particular towns. Specifics also focus on physical description, cost of living, housing prices, ease of shopping, medical facilities and retirement housing. We hope you will find this book not only helpful but also fun to sit down and read.

Each chapter addresses the following:

• Climate conditions in the area, including seasonal temperatures, relative humidity, snowfall, rainfall and sunshine.

• Recreational facilities and opportunities, including educational resources, museums, movie theaters and details about shopping convenience.

• Cost-of-living factors such as local tax rates, utility costs and other information gathered in personal interviews.

• Health-care facilities, number of doctors and specialists, dental care, clinics, hospitals (with specific services and accommodations), convalescent and nursing homes (with type of care and financing available) and availability of alternative medical resources.

• Senior resources and information sources, including senior center addresses and phone numbers so you can call for further information.

• Specifics on housing in the area, including single-family housing costs, apartment rental, senior housing (with specifics on financing arrangements, monthly rentals, services and facilities provided, nursing care provided, activities and transportation).

• Inside information to help you to learn about the community, what services it offers, the atmosphere, orientation and feeling of the town.

• Interviews with retirees who have located in the area to explain the rea-

Above—*Horseback riders make their way through the striking foothills of the Sangre de Cristo Mountains. Spanish explorers introduced the first horses to the Southwest in the 16th century. Photo by Chris Corrie.*

sons they chose their retirement locations.

• Key information sources and contacts so you can get more specifics and get them fast, as well as information and tidbits that only New Mexico residents know.

• *Retirement New Mexico* gives you the inside story on our state. We think you will find our story entertaining as well as informative. New Mexico is a rare and wonderful place to live. We hope to have you here in the Land of Enchantment as our neighbors and our friends, sharing the wonder of New Mexico. We wish to thank you, our readers, for making this book such a success.

*A WORD ABOUT TELEPHONE AREA CODES

Please note that at the time of printing (winter 2001), a new area code possibly was to be assigned to telephone numbers within the Albuquerque-Santa Fe-Los Alamos corridor. Although the new area code (575) was not to be phased in until summer 2003, we added an asterisk (*) to the area codes to be affected. Please check the number if the 505 area code does not work. The cities (and their local calling areas) affected by the change include Albuquerque, Belén, Bernalillo, Estancia, Los Alamos, Los Lunas, Moriarty, Mountainair, Placitas, Peña Blanca, Santa Fe/Pojoaque, Tijeras and White Rock. Also affected are the various pueblos within these local calling areas.

INTERNATIONALLY FAMOUS CITY

One of the most sophisticated and developing senior markets is found in Santa Fe, but the charms and attractions of northern New Mexico are also available in nearby towns, offering more economical living conditions that have been largely overlooked by many seniors. Depending on your lifestyle needs, health services and senior resources, the Santa Fe area offers choices and options sensitive to your desires and pocketbook.

Ben Maestas was a pharmacist in Los Alamos before he retired and moved to Española.

"There are tremendous opportunities here for recreation, sidelines and hobbies," Maestas says. He says proximity to Santa Fe allows seniors to participate in all the cultural options the city has to offer. The library system in Los Alamos fulfills his reading needs.

"The growing season here is a month longer than in Santa Fe and we're close to Albuquerque, too, so we have the best of all worlds," he says. Maestas thinks many people who left the Española area during World War II are now coming back to retire there. People from New York, Ohio and Texas are relocating in the valley.

"In fact when I go anywhere on vacation, I get homesick after about three days," Maestas says.

Above—*A man tills a field of crops on a small parcel of land in Chimayó. Many retirees to New Mexico choose to be closer to the earth and spend their sunset years in rural surroundings. Photo by Mark Nohl,* New Mexico Magazine.

ESPAÑOLA—VALLEY TOWN ON THE BANKS OF THE RIO GRANDE

The first capital of New Mexico was founded near Española in 1598 by Spanish conquistadores, but it was not until the mid-1800s that Española itself came into being. Situated in the Río Grande Valley 86 miles north of Albuquerque, Española (population 9,688) is blessed with low humidity and mild climate year-round. At 5,595 feet the town has clear winters, with an average snowfall of 14 inches. Snow seldom remains on the ground for long before the sun and brilliant blue skies return. In summer, temperatures climb to 90 degrees and cool quickly at night. Ten inches of rain a year falls, mostly during July and August.

Not much old architecture remains in Española with the exception of the Bond House, once the home of a Canadian-born merchant who became a merchandising success in the town. The house is now an art and history museum.

A farming, ranching and tourist town, Española also has many residents who work at Los Alamos National Laboratory. Española is well-known for the many "lowriders" who slowly cruise the main drag in their customized late-model cars. Sporting high-gloss paint jobs and chain-link steering wheels, the drivers of these low-to-the-ground cruisers have formed clubs that contribute to many community projects in town. A nearby Sikh ashram hosts international, interfaith events, including a summer-solstice celebration. Two hundred Sikhs live at the ashram near Española.

Every October a multi-cultural festival celebrates the artistic and cultural heritage of Indians, Hispanics, Anglos and people of other ethnicities in the valley. The festival is conducted at Northern New Mexico Community College, an accredited two-year school with vocational and academic programs.

Española, surrounded by Indian pueblos, has prime tourist country to the northeast and west of town. Santa Clara Pueblo, just south, is famous for its distinctive black pottery and also manages the Puyé Cliff Dwellings built by the tribe's ancestors between A.D. 500 to 900. Farther west, the tribe operates the Santa Clara Campground.

Fifty miles southwest of Española is the village of Jémez Springs, located in the steep and colorful Jémez Canyon, where the Spanish built a mission centuries ago to teach the Indian inhabitants new ways. Jémez State Monument is the site of a prehistoric pueblo. Not only is the canyon exceedingly beautiful— white and red escarpments and mesa rising from the valley floor where the Jémez River flows—but the mineral springs at Jémez, which can be enjoyed at a local bathhouse, are said to offer healing therapy for those suffering from arthritis and rheumatism.

Natural hot springs are scattered throughout the area. Soda Dam on the river gives evidence of thermal springs that still flow through this mineral formation. Renting a house in the area near the hot springs can provide a welcome and peaceful retreat. Rent starts at about $250 a month. There are also small resort cabins for shorter stays. Fenton Lake, farther up the canyon, is a man-made lake, part of Fenton Lake State Park, a popular fishing and camping retreat and a winter cross-country ski area. Twelve-pound trout occasionally are taken at the lake.

The area is served by the Jémez Valley Medical Clinic and a rescue and ambulance service. Seven miles south of town is the Senior Citizen Center, Jémez Valley High School, Star Route, Box 17, Jémez Pueblo, N.M. 87024; (505) 834-7337.

To the north of Española, the San Juan Pueblo allows visitors to fish at tribal lakes. The tribe also operates a bingo hall and casino. To the east is the historic town of Chimayó, home of the Santuario de Chimayó. The church, constructed originally as a family chapel, is the site of miraculous cures said to come from the holy earth over which the chapel is built. Pilgrims take the earth from a small well in a room next to the altar.

Española is served by a well-developed business community. There is a movie-theater complex and a neighborhood center with library, meeting facilities and gym. There are two pools in town, tennis courts, a campground and a cycle park. Annual June rodeos as well as other events are conducted at the Río Arriba Fairgrounds near town.

Seven mobile home parks are found in the area. Mobile homes rent for about $125 a month. Land is available near town at $7,000 to $25,000 an acre. An average 1,500-square-foot home is priced at about $75,000 to $85,000. A municipal airport serves the town.

Above—*Every Good Friday thousands of people make pilgrimages on foot to the Santuario de Chimayó, which they believe is a site of miraculous healing. Photo by Mark Nohl, New Mexico Magazine.*

There are seven pharmacies and medical facilities include the 80-bed Española Hospital, which has radioisotope and cardiac units, physical therapy, respiratory therapy, radiology services, home-health-care services and a laboratory and day-surgery unit. There are two ambulances in town and 30 doctors, five dentists and five chiropractors. For those who seek alternative care, there is an acupuncturist.

A 120-bed intermediate-care nursing home that advertises a home-like atmosphere is one of the main facilities for the elderly in Española. Twenty-four-hour nursing service, physician on call, balanced nutritional program, family counseling and physical therapy are some of the services it offers. The home accepts private pay, Medicaid, Social Security, veteran benefits and other financial programs.

Española Valley has more than 35 organizations that are active in the area. The American Association for Retired People (AARP) has a chapter and there is a garden club, Alcoholics Anonymous and Al-Anon Center as well as

Above—*Ancient ruins at Bandelier National Monument tantalize the imagination. Occupants of this Ancestral Pueblo settlement also carved out cliffside homes. Photo by Mark Nohl,* New Mexico Magazine.

the opera guild and a community-activities group. Major fraternal organizations are active in the valley as are the hospital auxiliary and historical society. There is the Española Senior Citizens Center, Apple Valley Estates, Española, N.M. 87532; (505) 753-2831. For further information on Española, contact the chamber of commerce, P.O. Box 190, Española, 87532-0190; (505) 753-2831; www.espanolanmchamber.com.

LOS ALAMOS—THE TOWN THAT SHAPED THE FUTURE

Thirty-five miles northwest of Santa Fe, 7,410 feet up on finger-like mesas, is one of New Mexico's newest communities, Los Alamos (population 18,343). Los Alamos means "cottonwoods," but most people know the town for what happened here from 1943 to 1945. It was called Project Y, the World War II code name for the secret laboratory that developed the atomic bomb. The city is still known for Los Alamos National Laboratory, a major research facility that is the town's focus. The Bradbury Science Museum outlines much of the work being done at the lab on nuclear, solar and geothermal research.

Long before the Pajarito Mesa was the site of this modern city, it was the location of Indian dwellings. The Los Alamos Historical Museum interprets and portrays the history of the area. The museum was designed by John Gaw Meem, a well-known New Mexico architect who also created the design for La Fonda in Santa Fe. Today's Fuller Lodge Art Center once served as the dining facility for scientists who came to Los Alamos during the war and was the base for a boy's camp before that.

Ten miles from town is Bandelier National Monument, site of Indian ruins and cliff dwellings in a beautiful and quiet canyon filled with cottonwoods. Other petroglyph sites and ruins abound near Los Alamos. Close by is San Ildefonso Pueblo, an Indian village known for its black matte pottery and burnished ware developed by the late, famous artisan María Martínez.

The alpine climate of Los Alamos ranges from winter lows in the teens to highs of 40 degrees. In mid-summer, daytime highs in the 80s are relieved by cool lows in the mid-50s at night. The area receives 17.8 inches of precipitation a year.

There are 18 parks, three well-developed libraries, a movie theater, two recreation centers and a country club. A theater group and civic organizations offer opportunity for community involvement. The recreational life of the town is centered on outdoor activities: hiking, backpacking, fishing, skiing, tennis and golf are favorite pastimes. Pajarito Mountain Ski Area has well-developed runs for all levels of difficulty. The town now has the highest elevation, indoor Olympic-sized pool in the country. Shopping is convenient, with five centers serving the town. There is a local bus system. Though railroad service is non-existent, the town has its own municipal airport linked to Albuquerque International Airport, 93 miles to the south, by commuter service.

Forty-five percent of the households in Los Alamos earned more than $50,000 a year in 1987. By 1993 that percentage rose to more than half. Los Alamos is an affluent and well-educated, scientifically based community that prides itself on the education it provides its youth. Single-family housing reflects this affluence. The average price of a three-bedroom home is about $130,000. About 550 homes are on the market during the year. Residential new constructions (wood) costs from $65 to $100 per square foot. Real property taxes are $24.46 per $1,000 of net taxable value.

Senior resources are well-developed. One 60-bed, intermediate-care facility serves the town. The Los Alamos Medical Center has 88 beds. There are 38 doctors to serve the city and 17 dentists.

The Los Alamos Retired Senior Volunteer Program (RSVP) for people 60 years and older provides senior volunteers to help with community services and programs. RSVP publishes brochures to detail specific services and programs. Write Los Alamos Retired Senior Volunteer Program, P.O. Box 488, Los Alamos, N.M. 87544, for further information.

Family Council, a non-profit mental health service, provides senior-program and outreach services, senior van service, homemaker aides and a daily tele-phone-reassurance program to call seniors living alone. Personal counseling services are also provided by the organization. The Los Alamos Senior News keeps the community well-informed of events and developments of interest to members of the senior community. For information on these and other services for seniors in Los Alamos, contact Los Alamos Senior Center, P.O. Box 488, Los Alamos, N.M. 87544; *(505) 662-8201. The center is located in Fuller Lodge. Write the same address for copies of *Senior News*. For further information on Los Alamos, contact the chamber of commerce, 109 Central Pk. Square, P.O. Box 460, Los Alamos, N.M. 87544-0460; (800) 444-0707, *(505) 662-8105; www.visit.losalamos.com, e-mail: chamber@losalamos.com.

SANTA FE—CITY WITH STYLE

Say the words "Santa Fe" and a host of images come to mind, expressing the particular Southwest ambiance of this famous New Mexico city (population 62,203) located at 7,000 feet in the shadows of the Sangre de Cristo Mountains.

Santa Fe's climate is influenced by the city's close proximity to these moun-tains. In summer, highs reach the low 90s but evenings cool to the mid-50s. Rains wash the city during summer afternoons until the famous Santa Fe sun returns the particular quality of light that seems to make the air glisten and for which Santa Fe and New Mexico are famous. Annual rainfall is about 14 inch-es. In the winter average snowfall is about 35 inches, but the snow usually dis-appears rapidly under brilliant skies and sunlight.

Given all the glitz and glitter of Santa Fe's reputation as the City Different, it is perhaps hard to remember the lively market town founded in 1607 by Don Pedro de Peralta. Santa Fe is the oldest capital city in the country.

Surprisingly, Santa Fe has retained its unique flavor despite all the publicity.

*See Page 21 for area code information.

Above—*The flowing, irregular lines of New Mexico's adobe architecture are delightfully complemented by the state's abundance of snowfall, especially in the northern regions. Photo by Chris Corrie.*

The town's heart is the old Plaza, site of many historical and cultural events. Santa Fe invites exploration of central attractions on foot. St. Francis Cathedral, with its Gothic style, is an architectural oddity in this area of low adobe colonial buildings. It was begun by Archbishop Jean Baptiste Lamy in 1869. Strolling the square, visiting Sena Plaza or walking up Canyon Road six blocks southeast of the Plaza to see the many artists' haunts brings a sense of elegance and leisure to any day. Restaurants, cafes and bistros can be found at almost any turn. There are 150 art galleries and almost 200 restaurants, featuring fare ranging from local *cocina* (kitchen) to haute cuisine.

Opportunities to explore the cultural riches of the city are abundant. A number of museums appeal to almost every taste and interest. The Palace of the Governors illustrates New Mexico history since its early beginnings as a colonial outpost of the Spanish empire. Across from the Palace, the Museum of Fine Arts houses a permanent collection of 8,000 works of art and often displays intriguing visiting exhibits. The Museum of International Folk Art southeast of downtown presents the visitor with a collection of astounding variety and depth, portraying toys, folk arts, textiles, costumes and exhibits that exemplify the richness of folk traditions. One hundred and twenty-thousand objects are displayed. Near the Folk Art Museum is the Wheelwright Museum

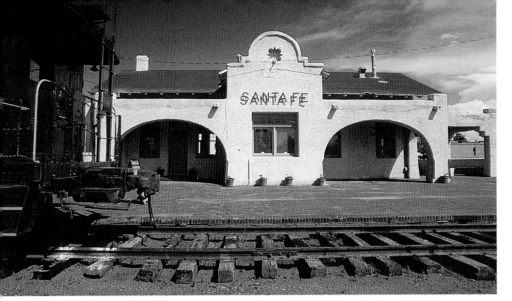

Above—*Still standing testament to a bygone era of transportation, the train depot in downtown Santa Fe today serves the Santa Fe Southern Railway, which offers tours between the capital city and Lamy. Photo by Chris Corrie.*

of the American Indian, which celebrates Indian cultural contributions. The Museum of Indian Arts and Culture, which opened next to the Folk Art Museum in 1987, interprets historic and contemporary traditions of the Pueblo, Navajo and Apache tribes.

In the summertime, Santa Fe offers a wealth of activity. Among the most popular events is the world-renowned Indian Market, attracting thousands of visitors to the Plaza where Indian artists display their arts and crafts. Earlier in the summer Hispanic artists show off their work in the annual Spanish Market, also on the Plaza, and cowboys and cowgirls celebrate four days of roping and bucking at the Rodeo de Santa Fe.

The summer schedule of activities is the colorful La Fiesta de Santa Fe, a four-day celebration on the weekend following Labor Day. The fiesta celebrates the resettlement of the New Mexico territory by Gen. Don Diego de Vargas and his conquistadores in 1692 following the 1680 Pueblo Rebellion.

Many people know about the Santa Fe Opera, in which internationally renowned artists perform. In addition, more than 20 arts groups bring theater, music and entertainment to the city. The Center for Contemporary Arts, the Santa Fe Chamber Music Festival, Desert Chorale, New Mexico Repertory Theatre, Community Theater and the Santa Fe Symphony are only a few of the many attractions.

Santa Fe is the site of a number of colleges that contribute to the cultural and social life of the city and provide a full range of adult and continuing educational opportunities suitable for seniors. St. John's College, the College of Santa Fe, Santa Fe Community College, the University of New Mexico Graduate Center and the University of Phoenix all offer programs suitable for seniors. Also, vocational and technical programs are available through the Santa Fe Vocational Technical School. Contact the Santa Fe Chamber of Commerce for details.

The city is served by a fine library system, including five public libraries. Fifty-three public parks and two semi-private and one public golf course provide amusement. Other recreational facilities include four indoor and one outdoor swimming pools plus 27 tennis courts. Hunting, fishing and river rafting are also favorite outdoor activities. Ski Santa Fe has a 1,650-foot vertical rise and 40 trails for all levels of skiers.

Living in Santa Fe can cost more than in other New Mexico communities. Median family income in the city is only about $38,000 (1997), but the average price of a three-bedroom house is close to $176,000 in town and $226,000 in surrounding areas. The housing market has been affected by people from out of state who have moved into the community. Real property taxes are the lowest of the 10 largest cities in the state, according to the chamber, with an annual property tax of about 5 percent. Several services provide financial help to low-income home purchasers in Santa Fe. The New Mexico Mortgage Finance Authority makes low-interest loans available for individuals or couples earning between $39,000 and $44,850. Funded through mortgage revenue bonds, the authority is not a state agency. Call (800) 444-6880 for further information. The Santa Fe Community Housing Trust serves residents whose incomes are below the median level. To qualify, you must have lived in the city for at least three years, this is your first home purchase or you haven't bought a house in three years. The trust is located at 500 W. San Francisco; *(505) 989-3960. If you need help with housing repairs, down-payment assistance, closing costs or low-interest loans and you are in the low- or median-income bracket, Santa Fe Neighborhood Housing Services might be able to offer you aid. They are located at 1570 Pacheco; *(505) 983-6214.

*See Page 21 for area code information.

Apartment rentals average $715 a month for two bedrooms. The town, however, is a patchwork of highly different income levels and it is possible to live inexpensively in Santa Fe. Housing bargains can still be had south of the city.

Well-developed transportation systems link Santa Fe with the rest of the state. Interstate 25 and U.S. 84-285 serve the town. Santa Fe has an expanding local-bus system, but the town relies mainly on car transportation or walking near the center of town. AMTRAK departs from Lamy, 30 minutes from Santa Fe. International-air transportation is available in Albuquerque, but Santa Fe does have a municipal airport.

Health services are provided by the 268-bed St. Vincent Hospital, a regional health-referral center and Lovelace Medical Center. Patient services at the hospital include urgent care, an emergency room, ambulatory-surgery center, diagnostic-radiology center and a cancer-diagnostic and treatment center.

Santa Fe is just beginning to develop its potential as a retirement location. There are some 10,050 residents who are 65 years and older. While about 45 percent of Santa Fe residents are upscale or affluent, only about 4 percent of the town's population follow a retirement lifestyle. Between 1980 and 1990, however, Santa Fe's elderly population increased 47 percent. Santa Fe is replete with retirement-living facilities. There are 12 retirement complexes in the town. One small complex is known as the retirement "bed and breakfast" of Santa Fe retirement homes. This small complex has only 12 residents who receive individual services 24 hours a day. Another two care centers run by a national company provide 24-hour care, specific longterm and short-term therapy and social activities. A facility located in the heart of downtown within walking distance of the Plaza, provides services for those who are independent and live in the complex's 134 apartments, and different levels of care for those who need nursing and 24-hour medical assistance. A unique and intimate family home for up to 10 residents, this facility guarantees residents will have individualized care and attention. Another complex in Santa Fe has 70 independent-living apartments and 26 assisted-care apartments near the Villa Linda Mall. This complex offers 24-hour care and two daily meals provided for residents in the communal dining room. Located in the center of town near the St. Francis Cathedral, one facility serves 120 residents with nursing and rehab for short- and medium-care as well as longterm care 24 hours a day. This residence provides activities, entertainment, organized excursion trips and many on-site services. Across from the rodeo grounds, another complex near many churches and the community college, provides all meals and care, assistance and activities for 14 residents.

Near the Santa Fe Outlet Mall, a center provides communal meals and activities, as well as 24-hour care in a homey setting for nine residents. Right next to the Plaza Resolana Center, an independent-living community features 35 *casitas* (small houses) and apartments. While services are available, this community caters to independent retirees. Also near downtown, another retirement community has 147 apartments. A third of these units are set aside for those who require assisted-living services. Dining, housekeeping and daily activities are also provided for residents.

An additional complex specializes in providing specialized services for Alzheimer's residents, with a specially designed wing for independent residents. Assisted living and those who need daily living skills receive a high level of care. This complex has 64 apartments having either one or two bedrooms. Residents receive three meals a day in the communal dining room and exercise classes, a computer center, hair salon and library are availabe. On the southeast side of town another complex provides independent-living cottages for 35 senior residents who suffer memory-loss problems (including Alzheimer's).

A valuable resource for seniors is RENESAN, a division of the International Elderhostel Institute that encourages learning opportunities for those over 50. Call *(505) 820-7895 for more information. For further Santa Fe retirement information, call *(505) 955-4721 or write Santa Fe City/County Division of Senior Services, Senior Center Council, 1121 Alto St., P.O. Box 909, Santa Fe, N.M. 87504.

For further information about Santa Fe, contact the chamber of commerce, 510 N. Guadalupe, Ste. N, Santa Fe, N.M. 87504; P.O Box 1928, 87504; www.santafechamber.com; *(505) 983-7317. For information on visiting Santa Fe, contact Santa Fe Convention and Visitors Bureau at Sweeney Center, P.O. Box 909, Santa Fe, N.M. 87504-0909; *(505) 955-6200 or (800) 777-CITY (2489); www.santafe.org.

*See Page 21 for area code information.

NEW MEXICO'S LARGEST CITY

The Albuquerque metropolitan area is an active retirement destination. While having all the conveniences associated with large cities, Albuquerque is only minutes away from rural New Mexico. Many retirement complexes have chosen Albuquerque as a preferred site. Others are interested in locating new facilities to the area.

Dan Garst was the vice president of a small manufacturing concern near Dayton, Ohio, when he first started thinking about coming to Albuquerque. He had a friend at Sandia National Laboratories and wrote him about jobs at the labs. Garst became a staff member at Sandia and worked there for 10 years. In 1986 he retired and decided to stay in Albuquerque.

"I've traveled over the U.S. and never found any place that had nicer year-round weather," Garst says. He loves the open Southwest vistas that allow him to see for miles in any direction, and he credits moderate costs as another attraction of the city.

"I love to go fishing," Garst says, "but I'm usually too busy." He's very active at the Bear Canyon Senior Center and regularly attends American Association of Retired Persons (AARP) meetings. Garst enjoys a lot of volunteer work and puts in time as a ticket-taker for the Albuquerque Air Show and the Río Grande Zoo.

Like Garst, many senior residents praise the climate, abundance of recreation, cultural and medical facilities and convenient

ALBUQUERQUE & VICINITY

Above—*Hot-air balloons inflate in the crisp early-morning air at the Albuquerque International Balloon Fiesta. Thousands of people attend the much-anticipated event every October. Photo by Mark Nohl,* New Mexico Magazine.

transportation. Some experts in town want the city to become another Phoenix. But they quickly add that they think Albuquerque can avoid the development problems Phoenix experienced since becoming a snowbird haven years ago.

ALBUQUERQUE—CITY ON THE MOVE

Be'eldiilahsinil, "Where the Sounding Things Are Suspended." That is the curious name given to Albuquerque by the Navajo. This odd, yet colorful term refers to bells rung at San Felipe de Neri church for vespers and Mass.

The church, remodeled several times, stands on the same spot as an original adobe chapel constructed at the center of the village founded in 1706 and named after the 10th Duke of Alburquerque in Spain by colonial governor Don Francisco Cuervo y Valdés. Several years after American settlers began to move into this small town near a place where the Río Grande makes a broad turn, they dropped the "r" and Albuquerque's history began to unfurl.

Now a city of 712,738, Albuquerque is ideally situated at the base of the 10,678-foot Sandía Peak, with the river bisecting the city. The commercial hub of New Mexico, the state's only metropolitan city has a pleasant climate with low humidity and warm temperatures that make it a pleasant place to live or visit at any time of year.

In January, temperatures range from the low 20s at night to the mid-40s during daylight hours. Humidity is about 45 percent in winter, gradually decreasing as summer approaches. By mid-July, temperatures approach their peak, reaching the mid-90s and cooling at night to the mid-60s. Humidity at the height of summer is only 22 percent. The sun shines 75 percent of the time in Albuquerque. Winter storms are brief and prone to stay in the mountains. The Río Grande Valley, where Albuquerque is located, is usually left untouched, but the few storms that do reach the city rarely leave snow on the ground for more than a day. During summer months, early afternoon showers refresh the air and break the heat. The dry desert air is a relief for those who suffer from breathing disorders.

Centrally located, Albuquerque (elevation 5,280 feet) allows easy access to Cíbola National Forest, immediately to the east of the city. In the same direction on Interstate 40 toward Cedar Crest, Sandia Peak Ski Area is only about 20 minutes away. To the north off I-25, Santa Fe is an hour away and Taos three hours.

The city is divided into several geographic areas. Along the river the North Valley area offers a semirural landscape, featuring large cottonwoods, open fields and sprawling homes. In south Albuquerque the quaint villages of Old Town, with its original Plaza, and Barelas give way to the charm of the South Valley. East of Old Town is the downtown core area and convention and government office center. Areas toward the mountains give evidence of later development and are divided into Northeast and Southeast Heights. From here it is possible to see the west bank of the river and the West Mesa area, dominated by several extinct volcanoes along the horizon.

Year-round recreational opportunities abound in Albuquerque. The view overlooking the Río Grande Valley is spectacular from the world-renowned Sandia Peak Tram, the world's longest single-span tramway. There are five private golf courses and five public courses as well as indoor and outdoor tennis, racquetball and spa facilities. Thirteen municipal swimming pools operate in summer months. There are a number of public parks in Albuquerque, and the Río Grande Zoo is the largest zoological park in the state.

A number of museums offer a variety of exhibits for visitors and residents. The New Mexico Museum of Natural History and Science focuses on zoology, geology and paleontology. It is located near Old Town, across from the Albuquerque Museum, which features art, history and science collections. The Albuquerque Aquarium features the world's second largest shark tank and an exhibit focusing on the Río Grande. In the desert such an aquatic center is a welcome relief. The aquarium is located at 2601 Central NW. Overlooking the river, the Río Grande Botanical Park, at the same location as the aquarium, has formal gardens and xeriscape desert flora with a pond and aquatic plants. The Indian Pueblo Cultural Center depicts the history of the state's 19 pueblos and contemporary works by Pueblo artists. Committed to preserve values and traditions, the National Hispanic Cultural Center of New Mexico features a number of programs and exhibits celebrating the richness and diversity of Hispanic culture in the United States. The new center is located at 1701 Fourth St. SW. The main campus of the University of New Mexico (UNM) is not only a showpiece for unique Southwestern architecture but also features an art museum, anthropology museum, geology museum and a gallery.

The UNM campus also offers many cultural events, performances and activities. The university presents a full schedule of courses that can be taken on a degree or non-degree basis. The New Mexico Symphony Orchestra and the Southwest Ballet Company are also top cultural attractions, providing a full season of classical music and dance. Music lovers will also appreciate the Albuquerque Civic Light Opera Company presentations. There are many live theater productions in town, including the New Mexico Repertory, which features fine professional theater experiences. Several local amateur companies are known for the quality and variety of their productions. The city has a well-developed public library system, with 16 facilities serving the area.

Albuquerque's calendar is crowded with events. Beginning in mid-winter and running through early June, you will find thoroughbred and quarter-horse racing at The Downs at Albuquerque, located at the New Mexico State Fairgrounds. In April, the Gathering of the Nations Powwow features colorful dance competition and arts and crafts exhibits by Indian tribes.

In 2000, Albuquerque's Triple A baseball team, the Dukes was sold and moved to Portland, Ore., after playing in the Duke City since 1972. In May 2001 the city's residents voted to renovate the city's 32-year old baseball stadium making it possible for the Calgary Cannons Triple-A franchise to move to Albuquerque. Thus, once again Albuquerque seniors will enjoy baseball. A

Above—*The downtown Civic Plaza in Albuquerque is a popular place to enjoy a meal, shop or attend a cultural event at the many nearby shops, theaters and restaurants. Photo by Mark Nohl,* New Mexico Magazine.

unique Albuquerque event happens annually when the Río Grande Raft Race matches 11 different kinds of crafts against each other in a helter-skelter 14-mile race down the Río Grande. Every Saturday during the Summerfest season Albuquerque's ethnic groups share their food, customs and traditions at Civic Plaza downtown.

The Albuquerque International Airshow in June gives visitors a chance to examine aircraft from various ages. Also in June, the New Mexico Arts and Crafts Fair allows 200 artisans to show their work at the State Fairgrounds. After July fireworks, the Cowboy Classic Western Art Show offers works by artists at the Fine Arts Gallery of the fairgrounds. In late August, the Charley Pride Golf Classic gives the town a chance to see professionals compete at the Four Hills Country Club.

Four hundred years of Hispanic traditional arts, crafts and entertainment are presented in the finale of the Summerfest series when the Fiesta Artistica occurs in Civic Plaza during late August. Then in September the New Mexico State Fair fills the fairgrounds with color and excitement. A month later the

Albuquerque International Balloon Fiesta presents the world's largest hot-air ballooning event, with breathtaking mass ascensions of colorful balloons filling the air above the city. Also in October, in alternate years, horse fanciers can see the International Arabian Horse Show.

Transportation in Albuquerque is the best in the state. Albuquerque International Airport is one of the fastest growing airports in the country. The westside is serviced by Double Eagle Airport, a facility suitable for private and charter carriers. Coronado Airfield serves the northern area and services private planes. AMTRAK stops at Albuquerque and highway arterials are well-developed. Both intercity bus service and city bus service are available. In November, more than 200 artists from all over the country show their works at the Southwestern Arts and Crafts Festival, a juried show that is one of the nation's finest events. Also in November, the Indian National Finals Rodeo takes place, featuring competitors from around the United States and Canada. The Christmas season is highlighted by the Christmas Eve *Luminaria* Tour, a fanciful trip around Albuquerque to witness New Mexico's traditional method of Christmas lighting. The Albuquerque Convention and Visitors Bureau has packaged several self-guided tours that begin in the city and display various aspects of Albuquerque and the surrounding area.

Housing is plentiful and moderately priced in Albuquerque. Single-family houses and apartments in all price ranges can be found throughout the city. There were about 3,600 active listings at the end of April 2001. The average price of a single-family home in April 2001 was about $150,783. This was about $7,000 less expensive than the year 2000 average sale price. During the first half of 1995, homes sold for an average $124,500, so prices have not escalated dramatically and have even decreased with an average sale time of about three months. Interest also declined from an average rate of 8.21 percent in 2000 to an average of 6.85 percent in April 2001. The Albuquerque Board of Realtors can provide you with information on the local housing market; *(505) 842-1433. They also maintain a Web site (www.realtorplaza.com) that maintains up-to-the-minute statistics on home sales in the Albuquerque area. There are a number of apartment locator services in the metro region that can provide details on location, availability and pricing the Albuquerque market listed in the Yellow Pages under "apartment finding and rentals."

In 1995 there were eight retirement communities operating in Albuquerque.

*See Page 21 for area code information.

At that time it was possible to provide specific information about fees and services offered by these complexes. Now there are over 60 retirement communities or homes in the Albuquerque region. Some of these complexes charge endowment fees or entry fees, others offer monthly rentals. Sometimes nursing care is provided. Citiesonthenet.com/albuquerque/retirement.htm is a good place to begin searching for specific complexes. These days pricing and services vary widely and the city's retirement facilities change yearly to keep pace with exploding demand, so it's best to call specific facilities to match your needs to specific communities. A host of senior services have also developed in the city in addition to home-health care. Doctor- and nursing-visit services, errand and shopping services, meal delivery, laundry, senior needs-assessment services have all cropped up since the mid-90s to provide for retirees in the Albuquerque area.

Seven multipurpose senior centers and 20 satellite senior centers operate in Albuquerque under the auspices of the city's Senior Affairs Department to provide recreational and social activities such as sports, health screening, arts and crafts, dances, physical fitness, meals and educational and cultural events. The centers also provide recreation to the homebound and intergenerational activities in public and private schools between youth and seniors. The Albuquerque Office of Senior Affairs is helpful and efficient in coordinating and offering the senior programs. Some of the services include senior day care, ombudsman advocacy for residents of longterm-care facilities, Retired Senior Volunteer Programs, Letter Carrier Alert Program to report uncollected mail, foster grandparents, minor home repair, Senior Outreach Assessment, home care, Seniors helping Seniors, adult-shared housing and Senior Citizen Legal Services. You can contact the office of Senior Affairs at 714 Seventh St. SW, Albuquerque, N.M. 87102; *(505) 764-6400.

Health services in Albuquerque are provided by a number of hospitals. The Lovelace Medical Center is a full-service facility with more than 200 doctors and a 100,000-member HMO plan. Seven urgent-care centers are located throughout the city. Kaseman Presbyterian, Northside Presbyterian and Pickard Presbyterian Convalescent Center also provide hospital care. Presbyterian Hospital offers many programs, including addiction treatment, mental-health care, home-health care, services for the elderly and occupational health. St. Joseph Hospital specializes in orthopedics, ophthalmology, neurology, neuro-

*See Page 21 for area code information.

surgery and general medicine.

St. Joseph Northeast Heights Hospital provides general medicine and surgical care, clinics for women and, like St. Joseph, provides 24-hour emergency and urgent care. UNM Hospital has a Level 1 Trauma Center, critical-care and inpatient and outpatient services. UNM Cancer Center is the largest in the state and treats all cancers on an outpatient basis. UNM Family Practice Clinic provides primary family-practice services. UNM Center for Non-Invasive Diagnosis is a magnetic-resonance research and diagnoses center. The Veterans Administration Hospital is a full-service hospital for New Mexico veterans. There are also three psychiatric hospitals in the city and more than 30 nursing homes operating in Albuquerque, including nursing facilities attached to retirement complexes and the Pickard Convalescent Center.

For further information about these and other aspects of Albuquerque senior living, contact the Office of Senior Affairs. For more information on services, facilities and activities in Albuquerque, contact the chamber of commerce, 401 Second St. NW, Albuquerque, N.M. 87120; *(505) 764-3700; www.gacc.org, e-mail: infospec@gacc.org. For visitor information, contact the Albuquerque Convention and Visitors Bureau, 20 First Plaza, Ste. 601, P.O. Box 26866, Albuquerque, N.M. 87125; (800) 284-2282 or (800) 733-9918, *(505) 842-9918; www.abqcvb.org, e-mail: armenta@abqcvb.org.

RIO RANCHO

Across the Río Grande on the West Mesa, Rio Rancho (population 51,765) is the fastest growing community in New Mexico. Originally, the site for Rio Rancho was grazing land that had been part of the Thompson Ranch, sliced out from the 18th-century Alameda Land Grant. Once known strictly as a retirement center because of inexpensive living and housing, the town now attracts younger residents as well.

At 5,290 feet, Rio Rancho shares in the general climatic conditions that favor the Albuquerque region. Its location above the river on the mesa, however, allows it its own variations on the climatic themes described in the Albuquerque section. Average rainfall is an arid 8.12 inches. In July, mean temperatures reach the mid-90s with lows around the mid-60s. In January, mean temperatures range from lows in the 20s to highs in the upper 40s.

The history of Rio Rancho is tied to the history of the New York real estate

*See Page 21 for area code information.

development company that launched the town. AMREP Southwest purchased 55,000 acres of rangeland on the isolated West Mesa, platted this area out and sold lots to retirees and speculators. The company held a number of promotional dinners, cocktail parties and slide shows on the East Coast to promote its development and persuade people to fly to Albuquerque to take a look at the vacant lots out in the desert.

Twenty years ago there were only 100 houses, rattlesnakes and a few wandering cows out on the mesa. Now there are more 14,000 homes and a well-planned city. Once a retirement town, now Rio Rancho's economy has boomed due to the presence of Intel Corp., which is currently engaged in a major expansion. Median incomes for the town are about $35,000. The area features moderate-priced housing. The average price for a three-bedroom home is $120,100. Real estate taxes on a $100,000 home are about $850 per annum (year 2000). The newest development, River's Edge, features houses priced from $93,990 to $170,990, with mid-range homes, but few homes go up for sale in this popular subdivision. Apartment building has exploded in the city. Average rents are about $700 a month for a two-bedroom apartment. A retirement complex with 220 apartments for active seniors (average age, 73) operates in this booming city. They have some assisted-living apartments, but the emphasis for the community is on serving the needs of active seniors who want to live in studio, one- and two-bedroom apartments. Arranged transportation and social activities also are features of this community. Another retirement complex in Rio Rancho has 12 cottages for independent living. This complex also has 80 studio, one- and two-bedroom assisted-living apartments. An Alzheimer's unit is also attached to the central complex. The town also has a nursing home.

There are 70 civic clubs, 17 shopping centers and well-developed recreation facilities in the town, including 11 city parks, three recreation centers, a public golf course and a private 27-hole golf course.

The Meadowlark Senior Center serves as the active focus for senior life in the Rio Rancho community, with a full range of programs for the elderly. One nursing home currently serves Rio Rancho.

In addition to health facilities located in Albuquerque, Rio Rancho is served by one hospital, two clinics, a county health office and two health-care centers. There are 79 physicians in town and 14 dentists. For further information on Rio

Right—New Mexico abounds with vestiges of the Old West just like this windmill and corral in a rural setting just south of Belén. Photo by Mark Nohl, New Mexico Magazine.

Rancho, contact the chamber of commerce, 1781 Rio Rancho Drive SE, Rio Rancho, N.M. 87124; *(505) 892-1533; www.rrchamber.org, e-mail: jdonovan@rrchamber.org.

BELEN AND LOS LUNAS— DEVELOPING RETIREMENT CENTERS

Thirty-four miles south of Albuquerque at 4,800 feet is the town of Belén (population 6,901), rapidly expanding as a bedroom community for Albuquerque. Still, Belén has many of the advantages of rural life. More arid than Albuquerque, Belén records only 8.1 inches of precipitation annually, but its temperature range is similar to that of Albuquerque, reaching January highs of 46 degrees and lows of 28. In July, temperatures climb to the low 90s and cool to the mid-60s at night.

No projects have been developed and specifically marketed here for retirees, but many seniors are finding this an attractive location for active retirement living. Valencia County, containing Los Lunas, Bosque Farms and Belén, is becoming known as a retirement destination. Chief among its advantages are proximity to Albuquerque, a calm rural lifestyle and reasonable housing costs. Most retirees own their own homes in Belén. There is a manufactured-housing community here that features its own recreation building. The community is gated and purchase of land and home runs about $80,000.

Los Lunas, the county seat of Valencia County, was named for the family of Diego de Luna. The Lunas arrived in New Mexico from Zacatecas,

*See Page 21 for area code information.

43

Above—*Magnificent sunsets are just one of many benefits of taking an exhilarating ride on the Sandia Peak Tramway, whose cables stretch 2.7 miles above the rocky precipices of the western Sandía Mountains. Photo by Mark Nohl, New Mexico Magazine.*

Mexico, in 1621. Some 125 homes go on the market per year in this town of 10,034 people. The average price for a new three-bedroom home is about $80,000. While there isn't a hospital in town, Los Lunas does have an assisted-living facility with 30 semi-private and private rooms. This complex will increase capacity by another 15 rooms in 2001. Currently, the complex charges about $60-$65 a day. Hospice, physical therapy and massage therapy are also available to residents. Currently (2001) there is a waiting list for this complex. Los Lunas has five doctors and seven dentists. There is one shopping center—no movie theater—a library and a senior center. For further information on Los Lunas, contact the chamber of commerce, 3447 Lambros, P.O. Box 13, Los Lunas, N.M. 87031; *(505) 865-1581; www.loslunaschamber.org, e-mail: llcc@nmia.com.

The main developer in Belén has been the Horizon Corp., which has built up the Río Communities subdivision. Townhomes, single-family houses and mobile home parks are all being marketed primarily to seniors. The average number of homes for sale in the Belén market is about 500 houses per year. The average price for a three-bedroom house is $75,000. Housing here tends

*See Page 21 for area code information.

to be somewhat less expensive than Los Lunas, which is closer to Albuquerque and the market here features newer homes in the $85,000-$95,000 range. Real property taxes per $1,000 of assessed value are 4.87 percent.

The recreational attraction in Belén is the Tierra del Sol Country Club, which has a 27-hole golf course and a junior-sized Olympic pool. The club also has a coed exercise room, tennis court, pro shop, athletic activities and functions planned especially for seniors.

The Belén community is served by the Valencia branch of the University of New Mexico, which provides an education focus for seniors who wish to take advantage of the proximity of a university satellite campus. The campus is a real center for this rural community and residents take great pride in the Valencia campus that often features events of interest to seniors. There are seven parks in the town and a library, a recreation center and a museum. Sports programs have been developed in the town. Belén has six senior centers. For information contact Valencia County Senior Center, 513 Becker Ave., Belén, N.M. 87002; *(505) 864-2663.

Health facilities are fairly well-developed. There is a 25-bed hospital and a nursing home with 120 beds. Twenty-five doctors and 11 dentists serve the town.

Albuquerque serves as the nearest commercial air center, but the town has a local airport. Interstate 25 runs by the town. There is no city bus service, but intercity bus service is available.

Community events include the Arts, Crafts and Trades Festival, an annual triathlon and Our Lady of Belén Fiesta. There are two theater groups, a musical organization and 50 civic clubs. Five shopping centers provide service to the Belén community, and there is one movie theater. For further information on Belén, contact the chamber of commerce at 712 Dalies Ave., Belén, N.M. 87002; *(505) 864-8091; www.belennm.com, e-mail: belen@belennm.com.

LAND OF GREAT SCENIC BEAUTY

J ust as the name suggests, the Enchanted Mountains is a spectacular region of alpine and subalpine beauty and splendor. Here, all the advantages of a quiet life away from the hassles and care of city living are available. Of particular note are the attractions of Taos. While the area is a prominent winter playground, Taos is an ancient community with well-developed resources for retired people who seek amenities and a surrounding community that offers cultural and recreational opportunities. While much smaller, Red River is also in a splendid location. Perfect for winter/summer recreation enthusiasts, Red River depends on Taos for health care and some of the other amenities important to retired living.

Curtis Anderson was born in New Mexico in 1910 but left soon thereafter. He spent most of his youth in Michigan, and he always dreamed of returning to the state. He recalls that he grew up listening to his father's stories about the Santa Fe Trail. After retiring as an economist for the federal government in 1973, Anderson and his wife went to New Haven, Conn., for 10 years. He studied and visited retirement locations all over the country to find the ideal place to relocate.

In 1986, a woman from Tularosa advertised in *Yankee Magazine* that she had a house in New Mexico to exchange. Anderson came out for a month and trav-

Right—An annual event at the Red River Ski Area, skiers carry torches while they traverse down the main town-side ski slope every holiday season. Photo by Mark Nohl, New Mexico Magazine.

eled all over the state. He came to Taos, loved it and sold his Connecticut home soon thereafter to move back to New Mexico.

"The air here is still very good," Anderson says. "We've studied the pollen count. The drinking water is very good and that's important." The climate is ideal, according to Anderson, who enjoys the low humidity, alpine Taos winters.

"I was brought up on the love of the Santa Fe Trail," says Anderson, whose devotion to Southwest history and lore has led him to become active in the National Park Association's project that marked and mapped the Santa Fe Trail. Taos retirement has made an ideal transition for Anderson, who has fulfilled his lifelong dream of returning to New Mexico.

RED RIVER—ALL-SEASON RESORT TOWN

About 40 minutes by car from Taos is the delightful little town of Red River, tucked away in a valley near the Colorado border, high in the Sangre de Cristo Mountains. About 13 percent of the town's 484 people are older than 55. At 8,750 feet, Red River is New Mexico's highest town. The tiny village took its name for a mineral imparting a rosy color to the river, which flows near Main Street.

The first inhabitants of the area were Native Americans, followed by trappers who explored the region in the early 1800s. Lured by word of gold strikes, Red River's population grew to 3,000 by 1905. Gold, silver and copper mines operated here until 1925 when the mines played out and Red River became a ghost town. The village was rediscovered during the

Depression when tourists came here to escape the Dust Bowl.

In 1958, work began on the Red River Ski Area, and with the completion of new Bobcat Pass in 1964, the town started to gain a reputation for being a family resort area. In winter, the average temperature is about 20 degrees and it snows: annual snowfall in the area is almost 132 inches. In mid-summer during July, temperatures are about 60 degrees. The ski area is located in the heart of town and has 58 trails, a quarter of them suitable for beginners. Another quarter are for the experts, while the remaining half are for intermediate skiers. Call (800) 348-6444 for information.

The town's calendar is full of events year-round, starting with the Winter Carnival in January and culminating with a torchlight Christmas parade in December. Recreational facilities in town include a movie theater, three tennis courts, a ballfield and a skating rink. In summer, melodrama is presented at the local inn.

The town is serviced by three part-time physicians, a volunteer emergency-medical-response team and two ambulances. There are no medical facilities in Red River.

There are 10 rentals in town. A one bedroom rents for $250 to $300 a month. Two bedrooms go for $300 to $350, and three bedrooms rent for $350 to $450. Mobile home park rentals, including utilities, charge $100 to $150 a month. For information on Red River, contact the chamber of commerce, P.O. Box 870, Red River, N.M. 87558; (505) 754-2366 or (800) 348-6444; www.redrivernewmex.com, e-mail: rrinfo@redrivernewmex.com.

TAOS—MAGICAL RETIREMENT TOWN

The origins of the name Taos (rhymes with house) are obscure. It probably came from a Spanish rendering of a Tewa Indian word meaning "red willow place." In the 17th century a local luminary by the name of Don Fernando de Chávez was called Don Fernando de Taos to honor him. In the late 1880s, because nobody could keep up with all the variations used to name the town, residents settled on the name Taos.

The location for the town is impressive. From the south, driving up the narrow Río Grande Canyon out onto the wide Taos Plateau takes the breath away as one observes the town to the north, flanked by the Sangre de Cristo Mountains rising above the gray-green plain. The town grew historically in three areas. Farthest north is Taos Pueblo, inhabited for 900 years. Then came Don Fernando de Taos, the current commercial district and, finally, more to the south, Ranchos de Taos, a residential and agricultural area dominated by the old adobe San Francisco de Asis Church, which has been the subject of many paintings and photographs.

Taos history is so rich that it hardly does justice to sketch a few brief outlines. Site of an annual trade rendezvous in the 1700s, trade center of New Spain, home of Kit Carson and retreat for artists in the early part of this century, Taos is alive with drama and color from times past. The Taos community is accessible by intercity bus or car. Air shuttles regularly depart Albuquerque International Airport, 131 miles to the south, bound for Taos.

The brisk and refreshing climate of Taos Valley bestows warm summer days on the area when temperatures climb to the 70s and 80s and cool considerably to the 40s and 50s in the evening. During winter, temperatures reach 30 to 40 degrees and drop to the teens at night. Occasional cold snaps take the thermometer well below zero. Precipitation ranges from 12 to 16 inches a year. Elevation is 6,983 feet above sea level. It mostly snows in January and February, and afternoon thunderbursts wash the town with refreshing and impressive rain displays in July and August. Other seasons are notably dry.

Above—*An aerial view of the state's largest river as it winds through the Río Grande Gorge west of Taos reveals the distant Sandía Mountains in the background. Photo by Mark Nohl,* New Mexico Magazine.

Throughout the year, Taos (population 4,700) has much to offer visitors and residents alike. Center of an active arts scene since the early 1900s, the town presents the work of many artists in more than 50 galleries. Walking tours around the colorful town are a regular feature of the summer season. Taos is a living museum of Spanish Colonial and Pueblo Revival architecture. Simply strolling through Taos offers a relax-

Above—*Inhabited by people for multiple centuries, the multistoried Taos Pueblo is a designated a World Heritage Site and is visited by thousands of tourists annually. Photo by Mark Nohl,* New Mexico Magazine.

ing diversion, with beauty and interest at every turn.

The Governor Bent House and Museum, home of Charles Bent, the first appointed governor of New Mexico in 1846-47, features exhibits on life in early Taos. Also of interest to Southwestern history buffs is the Kit Carson Museum, which recounts the life and times of the famous scout and mountain man. History of the Spanish and Mexican periods is captured at the Martínez Hacienda, a Taos trade center during those eras.

The Ernest Blumenschein House captures the excitement of the Taos arts scene and the characters who made Taos an internationally known art town. The Harwood Foundation and Library is a cultural center that researches art and artists of the country. The museum displays work by members of the Taos art community. Here, also, is the Harwood Public Library. Another arts attraction is the Millicent Rogers Museum, which displays Hispanic and Indian artworks.

Taos County parks, forests and scenic areas add another dimension to the area. Carson National Forest covers much of the county and is an ideal locale for camping, backpacking, hiking and horse trails. On North Pueblo Road, Kit Carson Park has a picnic area, tennis courts, basketball courts, baseball fields and playgrounds.

Driving tours originating from Taos take the traveler north to Angel Fire, Eagle Nest, Red River and back to town. Eagle Nest is a small town on a private lake of the same name. Charles Springer, a cattleman, banker, engineer and merchant, dammed the Cimarrón Canyon in 1919, creating the lake that is now a favorite fishing spot and an irrigation source for the valley. A visit to Ojo Caliente, 50 miles southwest of Taos, reveals five medicinal springs that have provided relief and healing for centuries. A resort surrounds pools containing arsenic, lithia, iron and sodium bubbles at a healing 48 to 110 degrees. A visit west of Taos to see the Río Grande Gorge and the bridge that spans it is also worthwhile. To the north and west of Taos up U.S. 64 past Tierra Amarilla is the town of Chama.

Chama grew where the Archuleta and Willow creeks meet and a railroad was forged over the *cumbre*, or summit, of the nearby pass into Colorado. The historic narrow-gauge railroad survives today. During spring and summer the Cumbres & Toltec Scenic Railroad takes visitors over the Cumbres Pass just as it did in the late 1800s. Chama has gained a reputation as a fishing and hunting location. In winter, cross-country skiing near town is excellent on well-developed trails. Each winter the Chama Chile Classic Cross-Country Ski Race and the sled-dog races in January fill the valley with sports enthusiasts and onlookers thrilling to the excitement of alpine sports conducted in the brisk, bright blue-sky weather of the Chama Valley.

The Taos area has developed an international reputation for downhill skiing. Taos Ski Valley is the closest area. About half of the runs are for advanced skiers, with remaining trails for intermediates and beginners. Annual snowfall is about 323 inches. Red River, Angel Fire, Ski Río and Sipapu ski areas are all within easy driving distance. Snowmobiling, sleigh rides and cross-country skiing are also favorite winter activities. During winter there is a monthlong jazz festival at the Taos Ski Valley, and many lodges have dancing and live music in the evenings.

The Taos Box offers spectacular springtime rafting in the Río Grande for many Taoseños, as residents call themselves. Later in May when the chaparral fills the air with the scent of sage, the Taos Spring Arts Celebration brings exhibitions, performances and studio tours to the town, highlighting traditional and contemporary Indian and Hispanic artists and musicians. In summer, the Taos Poetry Circus presents readings, workshops and events that feature nationally known poets. The Fort Burgwin Research Center offers a number of cultural programs and a lecture series emphasizing archaeology throughout the summer season until early fall.

In July, Fiesta de Santiago y Santa Ana and the Taos Pueblo Powwow bring drama and color to this ancient village. The summerlong Music Festival and Music from Angel Fire fill the town with classical performances of great works by the masters. Labor Day means the International Chile Cookoff, which allows famous chile chefs to compete.

There are about 200 homes for sale on the market per year. The average cost of a three bedroom in the Taos area during 2001 was about $191,000 with a median price of around $164,000, but homes span a great range (from a low of $39,000 to $1.5 million). Residential taxes on real estate are $30.67 per $1,000 of taxable value.

Transportation is either by foot (in the town's center) or by car. There is intercity bus service; charter- and private-air service is available. Shopping is well-developed in strip locations along the main highway into town.

Taos has many resources to recommend it as a retirement location. Holy Cross Hospital provides 42 beds and is an acute-care facility. A home-health-care service provides physical therapy as well. There is one retirement community in Taos, charging an entry fee starting at $50,000 to $150,000 (2001). The community has apartments (518 square feet) and classic 1,600-square-foot individual adobe homes. The retirement community charges monthly rentals ranging from $1,100 for singles to $1,500 for couples. They plan to build as many as 35 more individual homes in the near future. Twenty-four-hour continuing nursing care is available to residents. The community has a short waiting list.

Lifetime continuing care is provided in a 10-bed, licensed health-care facility. Monthly service fees provide most maintenance and twice-monthly housekeeping. Meals are served in a dining room, or tenants can prepare food in their own apartment units. One-, two- and three-bedroom deluxe apartments are available. Tenants supply their own furniture and personal effects. There is a library and activities room in addition to a dining room in the administration

Above—*Rafters take advantage of the annual spring runoff as they ride the rapids of the Río Grande as it flows through the steep-walled gorge west of Taos. Photo by Mark Nohl,* New Mexico Magazine.

building. Beauty and barber shops, laundry facilities and scheduled transportation are also amenities of the community. A swimming pool is a half-block away and there is a spa and exercise facility on the premises.

Two senior centers operate in Taos: Ancianos Inc. Senior Citizens Program and Cañon Senior Citizens Center. Both have the same address: P.O. Box 2449, Taos, N.M. 87571; (505) 758-4091. Contact the centers for further information on specific services and programs. For further information about Taos, contact the chamber of commerce at P.O. Drawer I, Taos, N.M. 87571; (505) 758-3873 or (800) 732-8267; www.taoschamber.com, e-mail: info@taoschamber.com.

FAIR CLIMATE WITH NO SEASONAL EXTREMES

EAST-CENTRAL HIGHLANDS

Retired ironworker Gene Roybal and his wife Pauline moved to Las Vegas, N.M., from Pueblo, Colo., because they fell in love with the area. Pauline, who is from Pueblo, says the weather and the scenery were two factors that accounted for their move. But one of the chief reasons they decided to relocate was the friendliness of the people they met in the Las Vegas area.

"It seems like you've known them for years," Pauline says. The Roybals are very active at the local senior center and have joined Senior Olympics. Together they play bingo at the center and enjoy fishing in nearby streams.

"It's a very moderate and inexpensive place to live," Pauline says about living costs in Las Vegas. The Roybals are typical of many people who have chosen to relocate in this beautiful part of the country.

The east-central highlands of New Mexico present the prospective retiree with a variety of opportunities to explore, ranging from extremely small out-of-the-way communities that offer peace and good climate with plenty of recreational options to larger locations more aware of the needs of retired people. This is a vast land with open plains, mountains and valleys. Water recreation is surprisingly available. The climate is moderate but differs from location to location, as does the scenic landscape and elevation.

54

Above—*Ute Lake State Park in eastern New Mexico near Tucumcari is popular among fishermen and water-sports enthusiasts, and nearby Logan is rapidly becoming a retirement haven. Photo by Mark Nohl,* New Mexico Magazine.

Though availability of medical and other services is a key concern for older citizens who are looking to locate in this area, a prime advantage is cheaper housing and lower tax rates. Some communities are just waking up to their potential as retirement markets and are now actively seeking senior interest for their communities. There might be golden opportunities for you to discover some real bonus locations that provide what you have been looking for in retirement location.

CLOVIS—EASTERN GATEWAY TO NEW MEXICO

They first called the town Riley's Switch, an intersecting line of the Santa Fe Railroad that joined the Belén cutoff and the Pecos Valley line. A railroad official's daughter was given the honor of coming up with a more appropriate name for this eastern plains town. Apparently she was studying the ancient history of France and so dubbed the town Clovis after the Frankish king who converted to Christianity in A.D. 496. The town is situated on a plain that stretches in all directions. Early Spanish explorers called this plain el Llano Estacado (staked plains) because it is believed they used stakes as markers to trace a route across this territory.

Weather in Clovis (altitude 4,260 feet) can be dramatic, with sudden shifts. From June to August, afternoon temperatures reach 90 degrees and cool off at night to below 65 degrees even in the hottest weather. Winter temperatures are mild, with an average maximum December through February of 50 degrees and an average night temperature of 25 degrees. Cold snaps seldom stay around long enough to bring extended periods of zero weather. Average annual precipitation is 17.64 inches. Most rainfall occurs between May and September and averages 2.5 inches a month, though it quickly disappears into loam soils typical of the area. Snow is infrequent and winds prevail from the southwest year around.

Cannon Air Force Base, seven miles west of Clovis, is home to 5,200 service personnel. Many military retirees find the town pleasant and friendly and have chosen to relocate here.

The Clovis Community College offers associate degrees and certificates of completion in academic and vocational programs; it has a paved outdoor-jogging area, an Olympic-sized pool and training track as well as lighted tennis courts. Area golfers tee off at Clovis Municipal Course and at the 18-hole Colonial Park Country Club.

Pioneer Days kicks off the summer season in Clovis with steer roping and a three-day rodeo. The Chile Cookoff, Mud Bog and Fiddler's Contest, as well as the annual Outhouse Race, tickle the fancy and begin the summer on the right foot.

In the 1950s, rock 'n' roll star Buddy Holly recorded his first hits in Clovis at the Norman Petty Seventh Street Recording Studios. In September, the '50s era comes alive when rockers of all ages descend on Clovis to celebrate pop music during the Clovis Music Festival at Petty's Main Street Auditorium. The Buddy Holly Memorial Convention, a '50s car show, parade and picnic is capped by the Rock 'n' Roll Hot-Air Balloon Rally.

Conducted in August and September, the Curry County Fair is one of the largest in the state and features exhibits and agricultural displays as well as arts and crafts, a Junior Livestock Sale and concession stands. Hillcrest Park Zoo and Ned Houk Park provide year-round outdoor amusement. The Caprock Amphitheater 49 miles north of town and the Lyceum Theatre in the city provide live entertainment. Ten miles south on U.S. 70, the Blackwater Draw Museum exhibits archaeological material and evidence of pre-modern man.

Houses in Clovis as of this writing (2001) were selling anywhere from $40,000 to $325,000, though the supply at the high end of the market was somewhat limited. An average three-bedroom older home sold for $95,000-$150,000, though newer homes were selling about $122,000-$130,000 (1,700-1,800 square feet). Three-bedroom apartments in Clovis rent for $675-$900. Clovis has a few mobile home parks; two-bedroom mobiles rent for $450 a month.

One hospital with 106 beds serves Clovis. There are 33 doctors and 19 dentists. There's a retirement home in town and a longterm-care nursing facility with 102 beds offering 24-hour nursing care. This non-profit facility is Medicare and Medicaid approved and the complex offers therapy and other services for residents. Another assisted-living center offers residents 52 rooms and eight apartments. Rooms (assisted living) cost in the $1,300-$1,450 range. Apartments for active seniors ranged from about $900-$1,020, and are priced for either singles or couples. There are no clinics, but emergency air-and-ground medical transportation is available. Amarillo and Lubbock, each 100 miles away, offer the nearest major medical centers.

The Baxter-Curren Senior Center and the Friendship Center provide some meals and other services. For specifics, contact the Baxter-Curren Senior Center at 908 Hickory, Clovis, N.M. 88101; (505) 763-2231. Information about the Friendship Center can be obtained by writing the director at 901 West 13th St., Clovis, N.M. 88101; (505) 763-5761. Information on Curry County Senior Meals Program can be obtained from the same address as the Friendship Center. Write to the director, Curry Residents Senior Association; (505) 762-9450. There are also a number of privately organized senior centers in town. Information can be obtained from the chamber of commerce by writing 215 Main St., Drawer C, Clovis, N.M. 88101; (505) 763-3435, (800) 261-7656; www.clovis.org, e-mail: cccchamber@3lefties.com.

PORTALES—GATEWAY TO THE EAST-CENTRAL HIGHLANDS

Nineteen miles from Clovis is the town of Portales (population 11,131). There's a sign outside of town that reads, " Portales is a town of 12,000 friendly people and 2 or 3 old grouches." This invitation to the community shows the kind of easy-going sense of humor that rules here in this relaxed little burg. The town was named for Portales Springs, six miles to the south-

Above—*Snow blankets the stone pueblo and mission ruins at Quarai within the Salinas Pueblo Missions National Monument south of Albuquerque. Photo by Mark Nohl,* New Mexico Magazine.

east. Billy the Kid used the springs for a watering hole. Cave openings that look like porch arches, or *portales*, are to be seen around the springs. The Pecos Valley and Northern Railroad came through but missed the small town that existed near the springs in the 1880s, and the railroad construction camp gave birth to the town of Portales. At 4,022 feet the town gets more rainfall than most places in the state, averaging about 18 inches a year. In January, average temperatures are a little below 40 degrees. During July it is about 80 degrees.

The pride of Portales is Eastern New Mexico University, which has its main campus in the town. The campus has a good library system with 293,000 volumes in eight locations, and music and theater programs at the university add to the cultural life of the community. Recreational facilities in Portales include a movie theater, ballfield, pool, two tennis courts, a golf course and an amateur theater group. There are two shopping centers and five department stores. Intercity bus transportation is available as well as a citywide-demand responsive van system. There is an airstrip for private planes, but for commercial service, the Clovis Municipal Airport is used.

Roosevelt County General Hospital employs 210 and has 42 beds. There is one outpatient clinic and a nursing home with 57 beds. Eighteen doctors and five dentists serve the town. For further information on Portales, contact the chamber of commerce, 200 E. Seventh, Portales, N.M. 88130; (505) 356-8541, (800) 635-8036; www.portales.com, e-mail: chamber@portales.com.

ESTANCIA—LITTLE TOWN AT THE HEAD OF THE VALLEY

Fifty-five miles southeast of Albuquerque, the small town of Estancia (population 1,584) is worthy of note. Located at the head of the valley that bears the same name, Estancia is a village that has become a bedroom community for Albuquerque. The valley is a kind of mineral bowl that trapped rain water to form saline lakes, a major attraction for ancient Indian tribes traveling here to gather salt.

Estancia means "resting place" or "large ranch." Near the Manzano and Sandía mountains and the Salinas Pueblos National Monument, Estancia is a natural playground for those who love the outdoors. The town is the seat of Torrance County.

Old-Timers' Day in June and the county fair at the end of summer offer residents parades, barbecues, rodeos, dances and fiddling contests. These events occur at the county fairgrounds and at Arthur Park, a pleasant cottonwood-filled park adjoining the fairgrounds.

The town boasts an active and well-funded senior citizen's program that provides daily lunches and transportation for seniors. For information on senior programs in Estancia, contact the Estancia Senior Center, P.O. Box 165, Estancia, N.M. 87016; *(505) 384-2354. For information on county programs and activities, contact Torrance County Senior Citizens, P.O. Box 48, Estancia, N.M. 87016; *(505) 384-5010.

Hope Medical Center in town has one physician to provide health care. Dental care is also provided. Full-hospital services are available in Albuquerque. The Estancia ambulance service has emergency medical technicians and helicopter backup from Albuquerque. The Public Health Service also offers immunizations and other programs. Each year the town conducts a health fair. Free testing and consultation are available through a variety of

*See Page 21 for area code information.

practitioners. For further information on Estancia, write the chamber of commerce at P.O. Box 1000, Estancia, N.M. 87016; *(505) 384-2339.

FORT SUMNER—PRIDE OF THE PECOS

On July 14, 1881, at the home of Peter Maxwell in Fort Sumner, Sheriff Pat Garrett surprised Billy the Kid in the darkness and shot the 21-year-old outlaw. The kid is buried between his pals Charlie Bowdre and Tom O'Folliard in the old government cemetery seven miles south of town. Now the town trades on the Kid's name to attract attention.

There is another reason why Fort Sumner enters the history books. In the 1860s, the Navajos were forced to walk 350 to 400 miles from their native lands to Fort Sumner. The route of the Long Walk was marked with the bodies of Indians who had died on the trek. They were then forced to occupy a government reservation at Bosque Redondo, where starvation, cold and misery decimated the tribe. The Fort Sumner State Monument four miles southeast of town is evidence of this bleak episode of Southwestern history.

The town has become an attractive location for retirees. The DeBaca Chamber of Commerce actively responds to information requests from those who want to relocate to the Fort Sumner area. The chamber is happy to refer prospective residents to retirees who have located in the area and will send you an information questionnaire. Local retirees will correspond to answer questions you might have about the area. Located in the Pecos River Valley, the town (population 1,249) offers a quiet village atmosphere from which excursions into dramatic and striking New Mexico scenery can be taken.

Precipitation ranges from 10 to 16 inches a year, with the rainy season starting in May. Dramatic and beautiful storms move southward across the county. Eighty percent of the rainfall falls from May through October, with 50 percent falling from July through September. The climate is semiarid continental with snowfalls averaging from 4 to 15 inches. Snow seldom accumulates and is gone after one or two days.

During summer, temperatures of 80 to 90 degrees fall rapidly to the 70s or 60s within two to three hours of sunset. During winter, only a few days have temperatures that fail to rise above freezing. The sun shines an estimated 3,300 hours a year, or 75 percent of the time. Average annual humidity ranges from 75 percent in cool morning hours to 35 percent in the heat of the day.

*See Page 21 for area code information.

Sumner Lake State Park is 16 miles northwest of town. On the west side of the lake, a retirement community has cabins available and serves as a retreat for eastern New Mexico. Boating and water sports are featured as well as fishing. Bosque Redondo Lake and the Pecos River also offer fishing and boating.

A highlight of the early summer season is the Tombstone Race at the school football field. For a $1,000 grand prize, men drag an 80-pound tombstone and women lug 40-pound stones while racing over an obstacle course.

There is one shopping center in town and one library—no movie theater. Transportation in and out of town is by intercity bus or car. Clovis, 60 miles east of town, has the nearest commercial-air service. There is a local airfield suitable for private planes.

Two senior centers provide services. For specifics, write DeBaca Senior Center, 510 Main St., P.O. Box 603, Fort Sumner, N.M. 88119; (505) 355-7365. Also providing programs for seniors is St. Anthony's Senior Center, P.O. Box 664 (Old Town), Fort Sumner, N.M. 88119; (505) 355-7311.

Two low-income HUD-FHA projects include 47 units in town. Mobile home parks are available and private housing is also for rent and sale. Existing houses can be purchased for comparatively moderate sums, but the supply, according to the chamber is somewhat limited. Recently (as of this writing) six MLS listings came on the market in Fort Sumner with an average sale price of $41,000. The median value of a single family home in town was $34,800. Land prices are quite favorable and many retirees locate manufactured housing on their sites or choose to build. Many retirees are buying lots in a 6,000-acre irrigated area adjacent to town and then build-ing or moving into modular housing.

The 25-bed DeBaca County Hospital has two full-time doctors. There is a 42-bed nursing home in Fort Sumner. The county hospital, clinic, nursing home, two doctors and dental clinic are all located in one central location comprising the Fort Sumner Medical Complex. Three ambulances are avail-able 24 hours a day providing EMT services for the town. An air ambulance flies to Albuquerque for emergencies. The Public Health Service also pro-vides services to the area and ambulance service is available.

A half-mile from town, the Fort Sumner Air Base has three asphalt runways to serve private planes. This industrial park and private-plane airport was developed during World War II and now provides transportation to and from the town.

The DeBaca Chamber of Commerce is very active in promoting the area to seniors who want to locate there, and the area is becoming increasingly popular due to its low housing costs, easy lifestyle and conducive climate. Contact the chamber at P.O. Box 28, Fort Sumner, N.M. 88119; (505) 355-7705; e-mail: ftsumnercoc@plateautel.net.

LAS VEGAS—AT THE EDGE OF THE EASTERN PLAINS

The dark, green eastern slopes of the Sangre de Cristo Mountains rise up behind Las Vegas and the eastern plains of New Mexico sweep away to the horizon. The Gallinas River runs through town. Las Vegas means "meadows." The original name for the town was Our Lady of the Sorrows of the Meadows, which was soon shortened to Las Vegas. On the Plaza from a rooftop in Las Vegas, Brig. Gen. Stephen Watts Kearny proclaimed New Mexico as U.S. Territory in 1846. The town (population 14,565) still has the feel of the old Territorial days, with winding back streets and original architecture.

A five-mile trip along Hot Springs Boulevard to the old Montezuma Hotel is well worth your time, especially if you suffer from rheumatism or arthritis. There, the hot springs will soothe you with 110- to 140-degree waters. The Montezuma Hotel once served guests such as Theodore Roosevelt, Ulysses S. Grant, Kaiser Wilheim and Emperor Hirohito.

Las Vegas (elevation 6,866 feet), a pleasant mountain town, is close enough to Santa Fe to be within easy driving distance and yet far enough away from city concerns to have its own life and local ways. The climate is pleasant. Precipitation is 22.62 inches a year. Summer highs reach 75 degrees with evening lows of 49 degrees. In winter, highs reach 52 degrees and lows dip to 15 degrees.

Proximity to state ski areas like Sipapu, Angel Fire, Taos, Santa Fe, Río Costilla and Red River make this a good location for winter-sports enthusiasts who also enjoy cross-country skiing. Pecos National Monument and Fort Union National Monument are nearby. In town, the Rough Rider Memorial Museum and Antonio Sanchez Cultural Center are good places to visit as well as the New Mexico Cultural Museum. The town has several galleries and six camp-

Above—*Springtime foliage returns to the trees and creates a pleasant setting in the Las Vegas Plaza, the site of many significant historical events throughout New Mexico history. Photo by Arnold Vigil,* New Mexico Magazine.

grounds within easy driving distance.

Average monthly rent for a one-bedroom house in Las Vegas is $400. Purchase price of a two-bedroom house is about $70,000-$80,000. A new three-bedroom house averages $90,000-$95,000. There are about 40 homes for sale on the Las Vegas market every year. A senior apartment complex operates in Las Vegas with six two-story buildings, each containing eight apartments. The complex also has 10 one-story apartment buildings. Highway transportation services the town as well as intercity bus service. AMTRAK provides service east and west daily, and the town has a municipal airport.

The Northeastern Regional Hospital is a 54-bed facility; 29 physicians are on staff. A rehabilitation center offers 13 beds for physical-disability care. A hospice and senior-care center also operate in the town. There are 40 physicians in town and eight dentists.

The Mora/San Miguel Senior Citizens Center at 500 Sabino St., Las Vegas, N.M. 87701, offers services to the county; (505) 454-0255. Also AARP is active at 906 Railroad Ave., Las Vegas, N.M. 87701; (505) 425-

7228. Contact the Las Vegas Chamber of Commerce at P.O. Box 128, Las Vegas, N.M. 87701; (505) 425-8631; www.lasvegasnewmexico.com.

LOGAN—ON UTE LAKE

Logan (population 1,094), located along the beautiful Canadian River in northeast Quay County, is about 24 miles northeast of Tucumcari and 80 miles north of Clovis. Because of the mild arid climate and the town's proximity to one of the largest lakes in the state, people are discovering Logan as a good place for retirement.

At 3,800 feet, the town gets 18 inches of precipitation a year and the sun shines 70 percent of the time. January temperatures range from 24 degrees to 52 degrees, while in July temperatures fluctuate from 65 to 94 degrees. Ute Lake State Park has picnic areas, shelters, mobile trailer facilities, overnight camping, docking areas, nature trails and an airstrip for private planes with no fees. The marina offers fishing and boating supplies.

Ambulance services in town have emergency-medical technicians and are in contact with hospitals in Tucumcari, Albuquerque and Clovis. There is one medical clinic in Logan. The Senior Citizens Center serves lunch five days a week. Ceramics, painting, blood-pressure checks and other services are provided by the center. You can contact the center at Box 592, Logan, N.M. 88426; (505) 487-2287. The Logan-Ute Lake Chamber of Commerce, P.O. Box 277, Logan, N.M. 88426, can provide you details about the town and further information; (505) 487-2722.

MELROSE—A FRIENDLY CURRY COUNTY VILLAGE

Melrose (population 736) was first called Brownhorn in the late 1800s. That is where the Brown and Horn ranches had their mailboxes. Today, about 60 percent of the town's population is retired due to the climate, low crime and moderate cost of living.

Wheat and milo are grown here. Melrose gets only 16 inches of precipitation a year. The high plains and dry climate, with moderate temperatures ranging from 39.1 degrees to 71.1 degrees, make it a good destination for those whose health requires clear, light air. At 4,599 feet, Melrose features beautiful sunsets and sunrises. Conchas, Fort Sumner, Ute and Santa Rosa lakes are all within 80 miles driving distance for water recreation.

Health care is provided within 30 minutes by car to Clovis, Portales or Fort Sumner hospitals. A retirement home in town was recently remodeled and offers 26 beds.

The Senior Center provides Meals on Wheels, noon meals, games, arts and crafts, and transportation to Clovis once a week. There are also dances at the center once a month. Contact the center at 528 Main St., Melrose, N.M. 88124; (505) 253-4261. For further information on Melrose, contact the chamber of commerce at Box 216, Melrose, N.M. 88124; (505) 253-4530; www.melrose.com.

MOUNTAINAIR—HEART OF NEW MEXICO

Located at the geographic center of the state, Mountainair (population 1,116) is situated on the Manzano-Chupadera Mesa Cordillera. At 6,510 feet, winter snows last in the high country only. Indian summer and cool afternoons in actual summer months are common in Mountainair.

For retirees, a plus for Mountainair includes its proximity to Salinas Pueblos National Monument (fascinating 17th-century Pueblo Indian and Spanish mission ruins), Manzano State Park and Cíbola National Forest. Tennis courts, two rodeos and the Firecracker Jubilee the first week of July are some attractions in town.

Housing is very affordable because at one time Mountainair had about four times the present population. A three-bedroom house costs from $25,000 to $40,000, but some houses in need of repair can be found for $10,000. Residential lots go for as little as $1,000. Double lots with utilities installed for mobile homes are available for $6,000.

Health care is provided by local physicians. Emergency medical technicians are available, but the nearest hospital is 45 miles away. A senior center located in the heart of town provides services. Contact Manzano Senior Center, P.O. Box 86, Mountainair, N.M. 87036; *(505) 847-2479. You may also write the chamber of commerce at P.O. Box 595, Mountainair, N.M. 87036; *(505) 847-2795.

SANTA ROSA—CITY OF NATURAL LAKES

Santa Rosa (population 2,744) calls itself the City of Lakes. At an elevation of 4,600 feet, the town is near Blue Hole, an underground river that sur-

*See Page 21 for area code information.

Above—*Farming and ranching are primary contributors to the economy in the Tucumcari area, where wide-open spaces and stock corrals are common sights. Photo by Mark Nohl,* New Mexico Magazine.

faces in a sump hole near the center of town. The hole offers scuba divers a 90-foot descent into incredibly clear water inhabited by carp, catfish and other fishes. Seven miles north of town is Santa Rosa Lake State Park, offering boating, swimming, picnicking, hiking, hunting and camping. Nearby Tres Lagunas is a nature lover's wonderland, perfect for hiking, camping, fishing and exploring. The Pecos River offers recreational opportunities as it winds through town.

Santa Rosa has a nine-hole golf course. Area hunting and petroglyph stalking are popular activities. There are also four city parks plus historic churches and government and commercial buildings to explore. In July, the average temperature is 77.2 degrees; in January, 38.9 degrees. It is dry in Santa Rosa, with an annual precipitation of 13.7 inches.

There is one hospital, the Guadalupe County Hospital, with 15 beds, two clinics, nursing-home services, two doctors, one dentist and a county health office. There is also an optometrist, two ambulance services and a rescue service. The Campos Senior Citizens Center is at 550 River Road, Santa Rosa,

N.M.; (505) 472-5248.

Several apartment complexes and seven trailer parks offer possible housing. For more information on Santa Rosa, write the chamber of commerce, 486 Parker Ave., Santa Rosa, N.M. 88435; (505) 472-3763, (800) 450-7084; www.santarosanm.com, www.rt66nm.org.

TUCUMCARI—ON THE EDGE OF THE EASTERN PLAINS

Fighting for the hand of Kari, the beautiful daughter of a local Apache chief, Tocom, died. Kari then committed suicide. Her father, in a tragic finale, also stabbed himself, and with his last breath sighed, "Tocom! Kari!" Hence the town derives its name—Tucumcari, or so they say.

Tucumcari, with a population of 5,989, presents a moderate, low-humidity climate year-round. Annual average temperatures are 58 degrees. In January, the average is 38 degrees; in July, about 79 degrees. Average rainfall is 15.66 inches and snowfall is 18.9 inches.

Conchas Lake, 31 miles away, and Ute Lake, 22 miles away, offer recreational opportunities for residents. Skiing is available within a two-hour drive. Rodeos, hot-air ballooning and the local Piñata Festival are highlights for residents. There is a country club, eight parks, two golf courses and a public library with 50,000 volumes. The new Mesalands Dinosaur Museum recently opened at Tucumcari's Mesa Technical College. Local commercial-air service is provided at the airport and intercity bus service is available.

Retirees in Tucumcari choose to live mostly in single-family homes. One reason is that housing costs in the area are quite reasonable, according to the Tucumcari Senior Citizen Attraction Committee of the local chamber of commerce. As of this writing, the folks at the committee say that railroad and trucking companies have withdrawn some employees from the area, leaving many homes for sale in town and in the surrounding rural areas. All the citizens of this friendly little town look out for each other. This community spirit makes Tucumcari an ideal retirement choice for those wanting to live in a small town that still provides lots of services for seniors.

The Senior Nutrition Program offers lunches and entertainment five days a week and a Meals-on-Wheels Program for those who are homebound. Vans can pick up seniors for lunch and shopping. Home Health Nursing, the Senior Companions Program, Lifeline emergency necklaces and daily telephoning to the ill and homebound all show the kind of care the community provides for its seniors.

One 43-bed nursing home offers semi-private rooms for $3,825 per month with no pre-investment required. Several assisted-living facilities operate in Tucumcari. One HUD-qualified complex charges $1,800 a month plus HUD rentals on a sliding scale. A 13-bed, assisted-living facility provides basic rentals at $1,600 a month, with hospice services provided for $2,500 a month. A 22-unit complex has one-to-three bedroom assisted-living apartments. Rents begin at $800 a month with meals provided for $20 per day.

The Dan Trigg Memorial Hospital has 25 beds and serves as a community resource for seniors through a Public Health Office, a hospice program and an outpatient clinic that will soon open. The hospital also offers Medivac service. Seven physicians, three chiropractors and two dentists provide health care for the community. The nearest regional health center is in Amarillo, Texas, 110 miles from Tucumcari. The EPCAA Senior Citizens Program at Third and Center streets, P.O. Box 1244, Tucumcari, N.M. 88401, provides nutrition programs; (505) 461-1914. The Tucumcari Senior Center at 523 South Third, Tucumcari, N.M. 88401, serves the city community; (505) 461-2307. Further information can be obtained by contacting the Senior Citizen Attraction Committee, Box C, Tucumcari, N.M. 88401, (505) 461-3093; or the Tucumcari Chamber of Commerce, P.O. Drawer E, 404 West Route 66 Blvd., P.O. Drawer E, Tucumcari, N.M. 88401, (505) 461-1694, www.tucumcarinm.com, e-mail: chamber@sr66.com.

INDIAN CULTURAL
AND TRADING CENTER

When Coronado came to New Mexico, he wandered about looking for the Seven Cities of Cíbola. Legend had it that somewhere to the north of Mexico were seven cities of incredible wealth and great civilization. Coronado came to the village of Zuni, which he thought was one of the fabulous cities of Cíbola. The word Cíbola marks many spots on the New Mexico map. It stands for a dream of discovering ease and luxury in the desert, a dream that today inspires many who have retired and relocated in our incredibly varied land of mountains and deserts to discover for themselves a land of peace, rest and opportunity.

One retiree who has found his life of peace, rest and opportunity is Gene Jeys, a former quality assurance engineer in the Voyager Space Program at Sandia National Laboratories. Four years ago Jeys sold his Albuquerque home and made the decision to move to Grants. He bought a home one-third the sale price of his previous residence.

"I fell in love with the mountains," Jeys says. "I grew up in Iowa and I never saw mountains until I was 30 years old." Jeys and his wife, Evelyn, are both writers and for them the inspiring presence of the mountains near Grants was a strong pull. However, Jeys studied communities as far east as Kansas before making a final deci-

CITIES OF
CIBOLA

sion; he compared lifestyles, home prices and proximity to his children. At the end of that period he decided Grants was the place for him.

Typical of many active seniors, Jeys' curiosity and desire to enrich his life leads him to continue his education. After retirement, he earned a bachelor's degree in psychology and has just been accepted in the master's program at Antioch College.

"You keep moving and doing things," Jeys says. "Being here by the mountains just sort of brings things out in people that inspires the best in us."

GALLUP

In 1881, when the railroad from the Arizona border reached the place that was to become Gallup, N.M., there was nothing except a stagecoach stop and a saloon called the Blue Goose. Two years later the town boomed, eventually even boasting its own opera house. Gallup (elevation 6,506 feet) was named for a railroad paymaster; coal mining and railroading gave the town its start. These two economic activities left their mark on a downtown that still evokes the late 19th century. Gallup (population 20,209) is also influenced by the Navajo Nation that lies north and south of the city and the Zuni Reservation to the south. Tourism and the Indian trade are current enterprises that keep the city afloat. It is often referred to as the Indian Capital of the World. The August Inter-Tribal Indian Ceremonial draws thousands for rodeos, parades, Indian dances and arts and craft shows. It is held at Red Rock State Park, six miles from Gallup.

McKinley County, which includes Gallup, straddles the Continental Divide, offering a wide range of terrain. Mountain alpine conditions and picturesque mesas can be found in the Gallup area as well as desert typical of the Navajo Nation. Average annual precipitation is 14.28 inches, with average yearly high temperatures at 64.8 degrees and lows of 33.6 degrees.

The Public Health Service operates a large hospital here to serve the Navajo Nation and Zuni Pueblo. Rehoboth McKinley Christian Health Care Services, for the general public, operates three multispecialty clinics that has 47 doctors and mid-level, health-care providers. The center has two hospital complexes with a 69–bed inpatient facility and a 49-bed psychiatric facility that offers substance abuse and inpatient care with outpatient capacity. They also have a licensed home-health-care agency, hospice and adult day-

***Above**—Colorful Eagle dancers dazzle crowds during an event at the Gallup Inter-Tribal Indian Ceremonial held every August. Photo by Mark Nohl, New Mexico Magazine.*

care services for seniors. There are three multispecialty clinics in town and three nursing homes. Thirty-five physicians and 11 dentists provide service to the general community.

A University of New Mexico branch campus offers two-year programs. An important cultural resource for the city is the Gallup Public Library, which has an excellent Southwest history collection.

Several low-cost, HUD-qualified apartments are available in the Gallup community, but there are no retirement complexes. Of the three nursing homes, one which is 92 to 98 percent occupied, still has no waiting list. Private financing, Medicaid, Medicare and other financing arrangements are made for this facility, which provides 24-hour care.

There are three senior centers in Gallup. Ford Canyon Center, which serves meals once a day, is at 908 Buena Vista, Gallup, N.M. 87301; (505) 863-6884. The address of the San Juan McKinley Seniors Inc. is P.O. Box 2728, Gallup, N.M. 87301; (505) 722-7266. For information on the Gallup Northside Center, write to 401 Joseph M. Montoya Blvd., Gallup, N.M. 87301; (505) 722-4740.

Gallup is served by both intercity buses and passenger trains. The Navajo

Transit system provides service to Farmington and the Navajo Reservation. There is a municipal airport. For further information, contact the Gallup Chamber of Commerce at 103 W. Route 66, Gallup, N.M. 87301; (505) 722-2228; e-mail: matthews@cia/g.com.

GRANTS

In 1872, Don Jesus Blea built his home under a grove of cottonwoods near Mount Taylor. He called his homestead Los Alamitos (little cottonwoods). The following year Don Ramon Baca and his family joined Blea. Eleven years after Blea had constructed his homesite, three Canadian brothers who were contractors for the railroad made their headquarters at the same place. They called it Grants Camp, later shortening the name to Grant when a coal station was constructed and a small town began to take root in the area.

In 1935, the name was changed to Grants. Oil fields near Ambrosia Lake were the source of a pipeline that went to a refinery near Grants during the 1940s, but the town didn't take off until Paddy Martínez, a Navajo sheepherder, found a peculiar yellow rock and thought it looked valuable. The rock contained uranium. During the 1950s Grants boomed as people from all over the country came to live in what became known as the "Uranium Capital of the World."

Located an hour west of Albuquerque, Grants (population 8,806) is no longer the boomtown it was during the height of the uranium industry, but the town has definite advantages for the retired person seeking good climatic conditions, beautiful scenery and an inexpensive lifestyle. The mild, arid climate in Grants provides residents with average temperatures of 50 degrees. Summer highs are in the 80s, lows in the 50s. In winter, highs are 40 degrees and lows about 10 degrees above zero. Average precipitation is only 7 inches.

The history and ambiance of a working uranium mine are captured at the New Mexico Museum of Mining in Grants. This is the only museum of its kind in the world constructed over a simulated mine complete with equipment. Southwestern Indian artifacts are also on display. Conference facilities and the chamber of commerce also occupy the building.

The town, at an elevation of 6,460 feet, is situated in the heart of ancient Indian civilizations. Modern pueblos surround the town and make an active contribution to Grants. This area is a wonderland for those interested in contemporary Native American life and customs. For the collector, the Grants area offers many opportunities to buy fine arts and crafts.

There's a lot of touring to be done near Grants. Thirty-five minutes east of town is the mesa occupied by Acoma, the oldest inhabited Indian pueblo in the world, a fascinating city perched on top of the mesa overlooking sheer cliffs above the desertscape below. North of Acoma, charming and intriguing Laguna Pueblo captivates the visitor with the spell of ancient past days.

Southwest of town about half an hour away are the ice caves, where subterranean airflows create a bizarre formation of perpetual ice at the back of the cave. Bandera Crater, a volcanic cone, gives an expansive view of the ancient lava flow called El Malpais. This national monument preserves evidence of ancient volcanic activity. El Malpais (the badlands) was a dreaded area during travel in the days of horse and wagon. A quarter-mile southwest of here is El Morro National Monument, the camping area and water pool used by conquistadors, cavalry soldiers, surveyors and settlers who carved inscriptions on the massive sandstone mesa. On top of the mesa are ancient Indian ruins that are partially excavated.

Thirty minutes south of El Morro is Zuni Pueblo. Coronado in his desperate search for the Seven Cities of Cíbola came here. While there is no gold, there are great riches in the form of Zuni cultural traditions. Each year in Zuni the mysterious and wonderful celebration of Shalako occurs, with its unusual dancers and fascinating rituals. Here, too, artisans create a tempting array of original jewelry.

From Grants, it is also easy to reach Chaco Culture National Historical Park, with its remnants of early Indian civilization. North of Grants is Mount Taylor, a towering inactive volcano. Picnic areas in Lobo Canyon or Coal Mine Canyon have individual campsites, facilities and interpretive nature trails. Snowmobiling and cross-country skiing offer plenty of winter fun.

West of town is Bluewater State Park and Haystack Mountain, a trout fisherman's paradise. Haystack Mountain is where Paddy Martínez discovered his uranium sample that changed the course of Grants' history. The reservoir has boat rentals, camping sites and picnic areas.

There are many recreational opportunities in the city itself: 13 city parks, a

Above—*The aftermath of an ancient volcanic eruption created the spectacular lava flows at El Malpais National Monument near Grants. Photo by Mark Nohl,* New Mexico Magazine.

golf course, two swimming pools, 11 tennis courts, nine baseball fields, a roller rink, a bowling alley and a movie theater. There are two shopping centers. Transportation is by highway (Interstate 40), intercity bus and passenger train service as well as commuter air service at the municipal airport.

Health services are provided by nine doctors, two optometrists, three chiropractors and three dentists. Cíbola General Hospital, 43 beds, provides intensive care and continuing care; a staff of local specialists and general-practice physicians offers service to the community. An 80-bed nursing facility has 24-hour nursing, rehabilitation programs and a home-health-care outreach pro gram.

The town actively promotes affordable housing, both single-family houses and apartments. Several apartment complexes can be found in town and there are two RV parks. Rents begin at $150 a month. Houses on the market range from $40,000 to $100,000. Subsidized housing is available.

There are many organizations of interest to seniors in Grants, but the heart of senior life is at the Senior Citizens Center, P.O. Box 876, Grants, N.M. 87020; (505) 287-7927. For further information about Grants, contact the chamber of commerce, P.O. Box 297, Grants, N.M. 87020; (505) 287-4802, (800) 748-2142; www.grants.org, e-mail: discover@grants.org.

SCENIC MOUNTAIN AREA

The San Juan corner of northwestern New Mexico is known for its splendid scenery and outdoor living. The Animas, La Plata and San Juan rivers converge near Farmington, accounting for 60 percent of New Mexico's surface-water volume and creating a fisherman's paradise. Ancestral Pueblo ruins near Aztec, the Salmon Ruins close to Farmington and majestic Chaco Culture National Historical Park nearby all fire the imagination with vivid pictures of ancient Indian life. The Bisti Badlands and Angel Peak typify geological wonders within a 15-minute drive from Farmington.

For those less active, the area affords good support. Aztec, Farmington and Bloomfield all have nursing facilities and low-income housing. Houses in the area are relatively moderate in price. The climate might be colder than some other places in New Mexico, but the high-altitude valley, mountain and desert scenery make up for a few inches of snow.

Newspaperman Dwight Payton says that he was living in Elsworth, Kan., when he visited his brother in Carrizozo.

"I was coming through New Mexico in August," Payton says. "We topped the hills out in Bloomfield and there was this green valley. It looked so beautiful. We thought we'd stop and check out the town (Aztec) just for fun." What started as an overnight stop was the beginning of Payton's longterm love affair with northwestern New Mexico.

He cites several reasons why he's found retirement living to be so pleasant in Aztec.

"You get sort of an in-between, mild, benign climate here. It never gets very cold in the winter and it never gets all that hot in the summer," Payton says. "The second attraction is the elegance and grandeur of the countryside. All the tourist sites alone would keep you going for a week or two. You're so close to the frontier out here. There's a little more of the old frontier hospitality and open-natured type people."

AZTEC—GOOD SENIOR RESOURCES AND SCENIC BEAUTY

At an altitude of 5,686 feet, Aztec (population 6,378) was named for the impressive ruins nearby, wrongly believed to be built by tribes related to the Aztec Indians of Mexico. Aztec Ruins National Monument preserves the ruins of this 500-room complex with its great central kiva, the work of the ancient Chacoan Indians. The Chacoans, part of the Ancestral Pueblo, irrigated their fields from the Animas River and constructed their buildings using incredibly skillful masonry techniques. The original inhabitants abandoned Aztec in 1125. Later, it was occupied by the Mesa Verde Ancestral Pueblo. In 1300, the site was abandoned altogether.

Above—*The rocky ruins of Aztec National Monument remind contemporary society of the complexity and ingenuity of the Ancestral Pueblo people. Photo by Mark Nohl,* New Mexico Magazine.

Within 50 miles of Aztec you'll find lake, stream and river fishing as well as water sports, hiking, camping and skiing in winter. The Cottonwood Campground and Navajo Lake State Park are nearby.

The annual average humidity in Aztec is 15 to 20 percent. The sun shines about 348 days out of the year. In January, about 9.5 inches of snow falls and almost 2 inches of rain. Highs are 39 degrees with lows about 13 degrees. By February, highs rise to about 50 degrees and lows dip to just

Above—*The Ancestral Pueblo builders of Chaco Culture National Historical Park aligned their giant stone structures with the skyward paths of the sun, the moon and the stars. Photo by Mark Nohl,* New Mexico Magazine.

above 20, while snow tapers to a little more than 2 inches. Snowmelt happens rapidly in the region. Temperatures rarely exceed the low 90s in the summer during July, the hottest month. Nights cool to the mid-50s. It rains most in August. Yearly rainfall averages 12 inches and snowfall is about 20 inches.

Conventional, Victorian-style and hacienda-style houses are available in and around town. Energy-efficient Earthship homes are also being built in the area. The single-family housing market ranges from $40,000 to $95,000. About 200 homes are listed each year. Cost of living is less than national average. The town has one shopping center. Aztec relies on Farmington for most air service, although there is a municipal airport with private and charter service available.

The Aztec Civic Center, 101 S. Park, Aztec, N.M. 87410, has varied programs; (505) 334-2881. Lunch is served Monday through Friday. The center operates a van service and lunch is also delivered to homebound seniors.

The town has several health- and life-care facilities. San Juan Regional Medical Center in Farmington fulfills health needs for those needing hospital care and attention. Fourteen doctors and three dentists provide Aztec with service.

A 13-unit apartment complex with an 80-bed nursing facility attached provides efficiency and one-bedroom apartments for independent residents. Housekeeping, maintenance and laundry are included in monthly fees. One meal a day is also furnished within the monthly charge. An 18-unit apartment complex for seniors offers no steps, grip bars or emergency lighting. Renters must be 62 years old to qualify. A similar apartment complex offers 30 units with comparable features to seniors. The same age qualifications apply. For further information on Aztec, write the chamber of commerce at 110 N. Ash, Aztec, N.M. 87410-1952; (505) 334-9551, (888) 838-9551; www.aztecnm.com, e-mail: aztec@cyberport.com.

BLOOMFIELD—IN THE CORNER OF SAN JUAN COUNTY

Bloomfield, with a population of 6,417, is a rural community located in the energy-rich Four Corners area. The town is an agricultural as well as a tourist center. The area offers extensive recreational sites, such as Navajo Lake State Park and the San Juan River, which offers great fishing opportunities. Angel Peak is a nearby attraction and the Nacimiento Badlands offer the visitor the specter of strange geological formations.

At 5,395 feet, Bloomfield has 12 inches of rainfall annually, highs of 40 degrees in the winter and 92 in the summer. Lows range from 16 degrees in the winter to 60 degrees in summer.

Residential tax rates for real property in Bloomfield are about $23.77 per $1,000 of net taxable value. The average price for a new three-bedroom home is $85,000. Bloomfield has a low-income apartment complex.
There are three parks in town and bookmobile service for library needs. This is a car-oriented town with one shopping center. There is a bus stop for intercity bus service. Farmington provides air service. There is a recreation center in town and a senior center at 104 S. Second, Bloomfield, N.M.; (505) 632-8351.

One 90-bed nursing home is located in the town (see also Farmington and Aztec). Two doctors and one dentist provide services to the village. For additional information contact the chamber of commerce at 224 W. Broadway Ave., Bloomfield, N.M. 87413; (505) 632-0880.

FARMINGTON—HEART OF THE SAN JUAN CORNER

Situated in the Four Corners area of the state, where Colorado, New

Mexico, Utah and Arizona meet, Farmington (population 37,844) is at the confluence of the Animas, La Plata and San Juan rivers. Sixty percent of the surface water in New Mexico travels through the Four Corners area, creating a lush valley that supports agriculture and nurtures wildlife. The valley is surrounded by high desert, rolling plateaus and mesas, with mountains to the north, east and west. The annual average temperature is 52 degrees, with monthly averages in January about 30 degrees. In July, temperatures average 74 degrees. About 8 inches of rain fall each year, and snow is 12 inches annually.

As the name Farmington indicates, the original reason for settlement here was agriculture. In the 1950s, discovery of oil and gas reserves caused the town to boom. Farmington, the largest town in the area, has become the cultural center of the Four Corners. To the town's west and southwest lies the Navajo Nation, contributing to the town both culturally and economically. Indian ruins and dramatic scenery are minutes away. The area offers outdoor activities of all kinds.

One of the nearby scenic attractions is Angel Peak Recreation Area, a 35-mile drive from Farmington. The formation is a 40-million-year-old accumulation of mud and

Above—Many water-related activities available at Navajo Lake State Park near Aztec and Farmington offer retirees plenty of choices for their leisure pastime. Photo by Mark Nohl, New Mexico Magazine.

sand that gathered on the floor of an ancient sea and subsequently underwent an uplifting, forming fins that appear to be the wings of angels. There is camping, picnicking and hiking. Canyon Rim Drive offers breathtaking views that natives claim compare to the Grand Canyon in their color and expansive beauty.

Thirty-two miles south of town, the Bisti Badlands is a federally protected area that features a geological landscape of barren moonlike stone, petrified logs and fossils—remnants of the age of dinosaurs. The imagination is spurred by the bleak sereneness of this world of stone, seemingly from another universe.

Above—*Ship Rock in the Four Corners region figures prominently in the culture of the* Diné *(Navajo people), who believe the formation is center to their creation as a people.* Photo by Mark Nohl, New Mexico Magazine.

Also south of town (67 miles) you'll find Chaco Culture National Historical Park, where the Chacoan Indians lived almost 1,000 years ago. Ruins of 18 major pueblos and a number of smaller villages have been discovered. Pueblo Bonito is five stories tall and has some 800 rooms spanning several acres. This cradle of ancient Indian culture seems to be haunted with the ghosts of that ancient civilization, which left behind baskets, pottery, jewelry and carvings of turquoise and shell. Overnight camping in Chaco Culture National Historical Park affords the visitor a real taste of the special wonder of this place.

East of Farmington, less than an hour away by car, is Navajo Lake State Park. Great fishing in the deep waters and three developed recreational sites offer boating, skiing and windsurfing. Salmon Ruins, just east of town, has 250 rooms of Chacoan ruins. Fifty miles northwest of Farmington is the Four Corners Monument, marking the only place in the country where four states meet.

The town of Farmington has many facilities of interest to seniors who might be considering locating in the area. Two public libraries have a total of 92,000 volumes. There are eight shopping centers. The Civic Center Theatre has seating capacity of 1,200 and banquet facilities to accommodate 700.

There is an abundance of sports facilities and entertainment in town: five racquetball courts, five handball courts, a skating rink, 17 tennis courts, two golf courses, three lakes, one bowling alley, three swimming pools, a new sports complex and 15 ballfields. San Juan Country Club also has an 18-hole course for members only. For the theatergoer, there is an amateur drama group. There are three museums and a city recreation center that regularly offers adult classes.

Three senior-citizen centers offer constant activities. The Bonnie Dallas Center is open Monday through Friday, 8 a.m. to 4 p.m.; Saturdays, 10 a.m. to 4 p.m. Meals are served on weekdays. Bus pick-up service can be arranged for city residents. Exercise classes, Meals on Wheels, Bible study, AARP meetings, potlucks, art lessons, blood-pressure checks, games, ceramics and dance practice are only a few of the activities. Contact Farmington Senior Center, 109 E. La Plata St., Farmington, N.M. 87401; (505) 327-7711, ext. 1380.

There are several support groups in town for grief counseling, the blind and those suffering from Alzheimer's disease and arthritis.

Senior health services are well-developed in Farmington. The area is served by the San Juan Regional Medical Center. In addition to hospital services, the center provides physician referral, a tel-med service to call for audio tapes on hundreds of health subjects, a wellness-after-50 class to assist in making healthy lifestyle choices and a Medicare-assistance program. There is an urgent-care center in town and several medical and dental clinics. Alcohol, mental-health and hospice services are available. Homemaking care serves the elderly community, and a senior-companion program allows seniors to care for others. There is a nursing-home ombudsman to help residents resolve conflicts with nursing homes in the area. A dial-a-ride with wheelchair lifts also operates in town.

The town has two nursing homes. Two homes also operate in nearby Bloomfield. Charges for the Farmington facilities are on a daily basis. Three low-income housing complexes in Farmington offer apartments to seniors who qualify.

Information on these and other senior programs can be obtained from the Farmington Chamber of Commerce, 105 N. Orchard, Suite 10, Farmington, N.M. 87499; (505) 325-0279; e-mail, fcc@cyberport.com, or logon to the Farmington Web site at www.chamber.farmington.nm.us.

HISTORIC AREA

In Old Cimarrón country the Santa Fe Trail days still live. This area features many tourist activities and outdoor recreation. Ratón is the dominant community and has more services for seniors than other towns. Clayton or Springer might appeal to those preferring a quieter setting. Colfax County offers scenic splendor and fairly inexpensive living. If you are a Santa Fe Trail and Southwest history buff, this landscape captures the feeling and spirit of the Old West along the trail.

Leona Rossetti was a barber in Wichita, Kan., when her doctor advised her to move to Ratón for her asthma. With her husband, Morris, a retired coal miner, Leona relocated and her asthma disappeared.

"We have the good climate here," she says. Leona feels that the key to her retirement success has been her willingness to stay involved in community affairs and maintain her active interest in developing friendships. She loves staying busy and enjoys being landlady of an apartment house she owns. The mountains and the ability to pick up part-time work are important to her. She also volunteers at the senior center.

"Come on out and try living in Ratón," she says, "I think you'll like it."

CLAYTON—IN THE HEART OF CIMARRON COUNTRY

Clayton, with a population of 2,524,

Above—The 19th-century Territorial architecture in downtown Ratón forever links this historic city to the booming railroad industry of that era. Photo by Mark Nohl, New Mexico Magazine.

got its name in 1889 when former Arkansas senator Stephen Dorsey came to New Mexico. Dorsey's reputation had been tarnished during a mail fraud scandal in which people who were promised daily service received monthly deliveries. With the help of his law partner, Bob Ingersoll, Dorsey got off and established a trading post at the site of Clayton, which he named after his son. It was the beginning of a town that today has a colorful past. With Ingersoll, Dorsey purchased a ranch 50 miles west of Clayton. There he built a splendid and isolated mansion, now on the National Register of Historic Places and open to the public.

Ten years after the town's naming, Black Jack Ketchum, robber and railroad bandit, turned himself in at Clayton to Sheriff Saturnino Pinard. In 1901 he was executed and buried here in a lonely grave. The Eklund Hotel, an 1890s landmark for travelers, still serves good food and is a reminder of these bygone days.

The town is situated at the base of some Rocky Mountain foothills called the Rabbit Ear Mountains, named for a Cheyenne Indian chief who roamed this area in the 1600s. Later, Indian scouts used the Rabbit Ears as a good position from which to launch raiding parties on wagons passing over the Santa Fe Trail. Wagon tracks from those days are still visible near town.

Above—*Clayton Lake State Park offers water lovers a cool respite from the beautiful rolling plains of northeastern New Mexico. Photo by Mark Nohl,* New Mexico Magazine.

Clayton remains a cattle town, as it was in the 1880s when a horrible blizzard wiped out cows and drivers alike. But today another chief industry involves carbon dioxide, used for injection into oil wells to stimulate production. The carbon dioxide comes from nearby Bravo Dome, a basalt formation that has trapped the gas.

Bisected by four highways, Clayton is an attractive place with wide, tree-lined streets. Intercity buses serve the city, which has its own airport. At 5,050 feet above sea level the town has a dry, mild climate with annual precipitation of 16 inches. The sun shines 77 percent of the time. Annual precipitation is 20 inches. High winds are sometimes common, but blizzards are a rarity. Average temperatures during winter are around 35 degrees, with highs of 48 degrees and lows of 22 degrees. In July, temperatures reach 90, with lows in the 60s. Average temperatures are in the mid-70s.

For its size, Clayton, which is the county seat, has a surprising variety of recreational attractions. There's a nine-hole golf course, a community swimming pool, tennis courts, softball diamonds, rodeo and fairgrounds, gun club and a number of city parks. Nearby lake and river fishing and good hunting within a 60-mile radius of town give residents numerous outdoor opportunities. People like to go camping and hiking at Clayton Lake State Park and Capulín Volcano National Monument.

Clayton also has a banquet auditorium and a small industrial park. The Wood Auditorium, a 618-seat facility, provides space for civic and school affairs. There is a modern library, with 14,029 volumes.

Health services are provided by Union County General Hospital, a 30-bed facility with pathology and radiological services, upgraded lab facility, X-ray equipment, an intensive-care unit and good diagnostic capabilities. Two general surgeons and an optometrist operate from their own clinic. Two general practitioners also provide services for the town. The Union County Medical Center, a primary-care general medical practice staffed by two physicians, provides service to the community and county. The town also has a chiropractic physician and an ambulance service that runs three vehicles. Air-ambulance service is available.

A 59-bed, intermediate-care facility, approved for Medicaid recipients, is located a block from the general hospital and physician offices. There is also another convalescent home in town.

New-home construction is about average for a small town. Many new houses use solar energy. A three-bedroom home can be purchased for as little as $25,000 to $30,000. Most homes sell (2001) around the mid $80,000 range, though some listings go for as high as $235,000 depending on location, size and amenities. Residential taxes are around $22.86 per $1,000 of assessed value.

Noon meals are served five days a week at the senior center to citizens more than 60 years of age. Meals on Wheels volunteers provide service to those unable to come to the center. Cards, pool, dominoes and quilting are a few of the center activities for seniors, as well as a daily recreation program. Contact the Clayton Senior Center at 19 E. Broadway, Clayton, N.M. 88415; (505) 374-9840. For general information contact the chamber of commerce, P.O. Box 476, 1103 S. First St., Clayton, N.M. 88415; (505) 374-9253, (800) 390-7858; www.claytonnewmexico.org, e-mail: cuchamber@plateautel.net.

RATÓN—AT THE FOOT OF THE OLD SANTA FE TRAIL

Old Ratón Pass was the original mountain or main branch of the Santa Fe Trail, the 950-mile link between Independence, Mo., and Santa Fe. The old route was too rugged for wagons. In 1866 "Uncle" Dick Wootton, mountain man and Indian scout, saw an opportunity to be of use to all these travelers headed west and make a little money at it. He blasted through the mountains, set up his own shotgun-protected tollgate and charged everyone who wanted to come through his pass $1.50. If the travelers didn't want to pay, they would have to go 100 miles out of their way to the east. In 1879, knowing a good deal when it saw one, the railroad bought out Wootton and established a line, along which the town flourished.

Ratón was founded at Willow Springs, a trail stop. At an elevation of 6,666 feet, the town preserves the feeling and atmosphere of the late 1800s in its downtown architecture. Walking in the area can be a real treat if you like old buildings. The town was not just an outpost. The Shuler Theater was completed in 1915 and still has its own productions. Walking tours start at the old Santa Fe Railway depot and visit 29 historic sites as well as Ripley Park, created in the early 1900s on land donated by the railroad.

Home to 7,282 people, Ratón is located on major north-south highway connections between Colorado and New Mexico. Intercity bus routes travel in all directions. AMTRAK provides service on the Chicago-to-Los Angeles line, and two, small air-charter services operate to the town.

During the summer, Ratón is warm and dry with cool nights. Highs are in the 70s and 80s with very few days getting up to the 90s. Lows are in the high 40s and 50s. During winter, it's usually mild and sunny with highs in the 40s and 50s. Lows can get down into the teens, with some 20-degree temperatures. Occasionally it gets below zero. Average precipitation is 16.34 inches, and the 152-day growing season is between May and October.

There are many activities to pursue in the area. The newest state park, Sugarite Canyon, is a heavily wooded and ruggedly scenic area about 10 miles northeast of town. The 9,000-acre tract extends into Colorado and has three lakes and a stream that courses through this unspoiled wilderness area. At the north end of town on Moulton Avenue, you can see the actual ruts made more than 100 years ago by wagons heading down the Santa Fe Trail. There is an old coal-mining camp and you can camp, hike and picnic at designated

***Above**—The historical Shuler Theater in Ratón is a fabulous venue for events attended by the cultural minded of northeastern New Mexico . Photo by Mark Nohl, New Mexico Magazine.*

sites. South of town the rock-walled Cimarrón Canyon is a beautiful drive. Just south of Cimarrón, the Philmont Scout Ranch is the summer home of Boy Scouts from around the world.

Ratón has a full-events calendar that starts with the Santa Fe Trail Rendezvous in early summer and ending in a City of Bethlehem Light Display during the Christmas season. There is a nine-hole municipal golf course, a roller rink, 12 tennis courts, a municipal outdoor pool, two health clubs and a country club with pool. The Arthur Johnson Library has more than 31,500 books. One major shopping center and several smaller business centers service the town. Some 150 houses are listed on the market each year. New three-bedroom houses ranged from $65,000 to $80,000 in 2001. Property taxes are assessed per $1,000 of value at $32.42. There are also four mobile home parks around the small city.

Health services are well-developed. There are two local health clubs in town. Thirteen doctors provide health-care services for Ratón. There are five dentists, two chiropractors, one optometrist, two opticians, massage therapist, acupuncturist and a podiatrist. Miners Colfax Medical Center is a 48-bed, acute-care facility housed in two separate locations. Inpatient and outpatient

Above—*There is no doubt these officers' quarters have seen better days at Fort Union National Monument, from which the U.S. Army protected travelers on the Santa Fe Trail. Photo by Mark Nohl,* New Mexico Magazine.

services, same-day surgery, cancer treatment, pulmonary care, special-care unit, surgical and medical services, lab, cardio-pulmonary care, black-lung diagnosis and treatment, respiratory clinic, CAT-scanner services, 24-hour emergency room, Alzheimer's unit, therapy center and an exercise center are some of the services provided by the center.

A nursing-home facility in Ratón provides longterm care and an Alzheimer's unit and treatment for the elderly. Services are free for those persons eligible. Sick and convalescence services, 24-hour nursing, personal care and planned activities are all available. The facility is Medicaid-eligible. Longterm and respite care as well as 24-hour nursing are provided. Medicaid, private and Veterans Administration financing are available. The facility has capacity for 10 intermediate-care patients and 60 residents.

The Ratón Senior Center, provides a full range of activities for seniors: 116 S. Third, Ratón, N.M. 87740; (505) 445-3278. A 15-passenger bus transports participants to and from the center for activities and meals as well as visits to regional senior centers. The center sponsors a Meals on Wheels program.

For information about Ratón, contact the chamber of commerce at P.O. Box 1211, 100 Clayton Road, Ratón, N.M. 87740; (505) 445-3689, (800) 638-6161; www.raton.com, e-mail: chamber@raton.com.

SPRINGER—WHERE THE OLD SANTA FE TRAIL LIVES

Springer was a watering hole on the Santa Fe Trail. Then it became the seat of Colfax County, but not for long. In the late 1880s Ratón fought with Springer for the honor of being the county seat and won. A remnant of those days is the splendid courthouse located in Springer, now a museum commemorating the Santa Fe Trail.

The Dorsey Mansion (discussed earlier in this chapter) is northeast of Springer. It is now a bed and breakfast that conducts tours through the old house. The 10,000-square-foot, 36-room mansion is the ideal setting for elegant, if not lonesome, living.

At 5,857 feet, Springer has a pleasant climate with average July temperatures a little above 70 degrees. In January, temperatures hover around 30 degrees. Annual snowfall approaches 30 inches, while rainfall is about 16 inches. This small town of 1,285 people has intercity bus service and interconnecting charter-air service with Ratón from the municipal airport.

The town offers recreational opportunities with a movie theater, skating rink, ballfield, two swimming pools, a couple of tennis courts and an all-weather track. Fishing lakes and streams, as well as camping and hunting are within 25 to 50 miles of town (see Ratón). Cost of living in the community is about average for the state. Housing is a little cheaper than elsewhere, but natural gas is more expensive. Single-family housing costs somewhere between $20,000 and $80,000. There are 684 units in town. Rentals are scarce, but a one bedroom rents for $264, a two bedroom for $308 and a three bedroom for $377. Subsidized housing is available. There are two mobile home parks and one RV park.

Medical facilities are available in Ratón. There are two doctors and a dentist in town. Springer ambulance services provide ground and air service.

Springer has a nursing home and a senior center that conducts tours around the state and provides medical testing. There are social groups, community clubs and several fraternal organizations in town. Contact the Springer Senior Center at P.O. Box 143, Springer, N.M. 87747; (505) 483-5900. For further information on Springer, contact the chamber of commerce, Box 323, Springer, N.M. 87747; (505) 483-2998.

A PLACE IN THE SUN
MILD CLIMATE WITHOUT EXTREMES

The Middle Río Grande Valley features two retirement destinations that are gaining in popularity: Socorro and Truth or Consequences. Socorro's retirement market is not as developed as that of Truth or Consequences, but it has a genuine historical charm and features a lot to do in the area.

Socorro County, located in the northern sector of the Middle Río Grande Valley, has a variety of desert and mountain terrain and preserves an unpretentious historical awareness that is a real pleasure. For the nature lover, the town is near several key areas of interest. The Bosque del Apache is a forest area and marsh-lake preserve for thousands of birds. The area at one time was a prime camping place for the Apache Indians.

Area topography features mesquite and creosote brush that cover rolling plains between rugged desert mountains. Characterized by expansive vistas and azure skies, it is a wild and beautiful landscape.

A mishap brought retired aerospace logistics analyst Pete Sepe to the Socorro area. He was driving through town a few years ago when his pickup broke down. While having it repaired at a local garage, he struck up a friendship with the owner. For vacation the next summer, he headed back to the area from his home in San

Above—*Migrating waterfowl make their annual winter pit stop along the Río Grande at the Bosque del Apache National Wildlife Refuge near Socorro. Photo by Mark Nohl,* New Mexico Magazine.

Diego, where he had been in retirement for five years. Sepe started to make friends. Now he has a house in Socorro and property in nearby Magdalena. "I like the uncrowded conditions," he says. "I like the character of the area, the people and the Hispanic culture. The air is a lot cleaner here than in California. There's less pressure, less hustle-bustle."

At the southern end of the Middle Río Grande region is Truth or Consequences, a small town that has developed a well-deserved reputation for serving seniors. Key attractions in "T or C," as the town is called by natives, are thermal baths that are soothing to arthritis and rheumatism sufferers, and nearby reservoirs that offer year-round recreational possibilities. This is a growing retirement location that is appealing if you want a desert hideaway that offers on-the-water activities.

While the Middle Río Grande features four seasons, activities here can be undertaken in any season. The climate is brisk and dry in the winter, and in the summer daytime dry heat cools at night. Always pleasant and never humid, the Middle Río Grande Valley is becoming ever-more popular as a retirement destination.

SOCORRO—GATEWAY TO THE OLD WEST

Near the Río Grande, a couple of hundred feet above the marshes of the lower riverbed, Franciscan fathers planted the first grapes in New Mexico and established the Mission of San Miguel. The church of San Miguel, begun in 1819 and completed in 1821, stands on the site of the original 17th-century mission. Featuring massive adobe walls, large carved vigas and corbelled arches, the church is just one of the architectural treats awaiting the visitor or resident who wishes to take a leisurely stroll around Socorro.

The original town of Socorro established in the early to mid-1600s survived until the Pueblo Revolt of 1680, when it was abandoned. During the early 1800s, land grants were given to 21 families who extended control of the Socorro area to the Oscura (dark) Mountains, south to Bosque del Apache and west to the Magdalena Mountains.

Socorro is located in a wide, fertile valley with water flowing from nearby mountains and is blessed with mineral wealth. During the late 1800s, Socorro was the largest town in the New Mexico Territory. Cattle, silver, flour and wine all came from Socorro. In the 1880s, Socorro County also witnessed the exploits of lawman Elfego Baca, an early associate of Billy the Kid. According to area lore, when Baca was only 18 years old, he stood off 80 Texas and English cowboys in a 33-hour gunbattle in which more than 4,000 shots were fired.

Contemporary Socorro (population 8,877) bears the traces of its early history as evidenced in its renowned architecture. The old town near the center of Socorro still features an arrangement of irregular streets radiating from the Plaza. Due to successive stages of boom and growth, houses near the town's core feature various eras of redecoration, making the town a paradise for observing New Mexico historical architecture.

Territorial-style houses alternate with Victorian and Queen Anne red brick houses built during the late 1880s and 1890s. Mission-style houses can be seen near the town's center. Typical of the Mission style, the Val Verde, a 60-room luxury hotel constructed in 1919, was recently remodeled. All of these architectural remnants can be toured by foot within easy access of the Plaza.

Socorro's climate is typical of conditions encountered in high-desert elevations. Average highs and lows in January range from 25 degrees to a pleasant 55 degrees. In July temperatures go from 61 degrees to 93 degrees. Nights cool off during summer months due to the low humidity. Average precipitation is only 8.8 inches and average snowfall is 6.3 inches. The Socorro area is a treasure chest for those who are attuned to the outdoors and who have well-developed historical interests and are curious about nature.

In 1939, the Fish and Wildlife Service established the Bosque del Apache Wildlife Refuge south of Socorro, today a 57,000-acre habitat for 300 bird species and more than 400 amphibians, reptiles and mammals. Hundreds of thousands of birds visit the area, rising from the 1,500-acre area where sorghum, winter wheat and millet are planted in shallow water to attract them. Cranes, herons and geese cloud the air and rest majestically in ponds and long grasses. A self-guided tour takes an hour and a half by car. Visitors can observe eagles, whooping cranes, coyotes, deer and sandhill cranes; observation towers in parking areas offer great views.

The Cíbola National Forest north and south of Magdalena features campgrounds and picnic areas. The forest is a hiker's dream. The ranger station in Magdalena provides complete information on facilities to be found in this part of Cíbola National Forest. You can contact the Magdalena Ranger Station at P.O. Box 45, Magdalena, N.M. 87825; (505) 854-2281.

The northern access to Elephant Butte State Park is about 30 miles south of Socorro (see the Truth or Consequences section later in this chapter for more information on Elephant Butte). RV hookups are available. Boating and bass fishing here are excellent.

If you are a golfer, Socorro has one of the best 18-hole courses in the state. The New Mexico Tech Golf Course is home of the annual Hilton Open and the Chile Chase. Tournaments go from April through November. Because of Socorro's mild climate, it is possible to play golf year-round. Tennis courts and indoor swimming are also available. The course is located on the campus of the New Mexico Institute of Mining and Technology, a high-quality institution specializing in science and mineral engineering. Tech is known as a research center for atmospheric, earth and materials sciences.

If you have an interest in geology, the Mineral Museum, located on the Tech campus, has more than 10,000 mineral specimens and is open Monday through Friday from 8 a.m. to 5 p.m.

Tech also operates the Langmuir Laboratory, an hour's drive from town. Open from June through August, the laboratory studies thunderclouds and light-

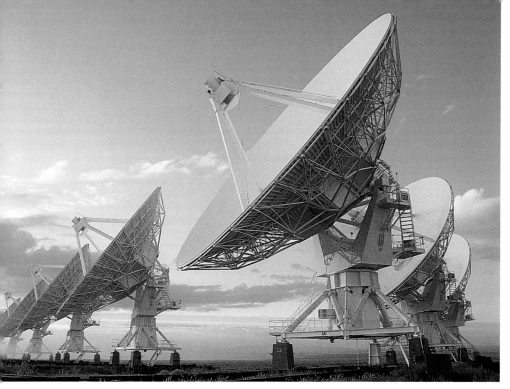

Above—*Futuristic radio telescopes scan the heavens at the Very Large Array (VLA) National Radio Astronomy Observatory near Magdalena. Photo by Mark Nohl,* New Mexico Magazine.

ning formation. The lab was featured on a "Nova" PBS broadcast about atmospheric electricity.

Another site of great interest to the scientifically minded can be found 54 miles west of Socorro. The Very Large Array (VLA), an impressive arrangement of 27 giant antenna dishes on the Plains of San Agustín, investigates the physics of radio sources beyond the Milky Way. The VLA is one part of the National Radio Astronomy Observatory, which includes the Very Long Baseline Array (VLBA), a series of radio antennas stretching from St. Croix to Hawaii and throughout the United States. Data from these technical facilities are compiled by computers located in Socorro.

Macey Center on the Tech campus is a complete conference area with an 800-seat theater. The New Mexico Tech Performing Arts Series provides winter entertainment. Art exhibits and other shows are displayed throughout the year.

In western Socorro County the Alamo Navajo Reservation is home to 1,400 Navajos. The reservation invites members of the public to visit on special occasions. Information about these events can be obtained by phoning the Alamo Navajo Chapter office at (505) 854-2686.

Socorro offers a haven for sightseers. The town is a gateway to Old West country. One of the most interesting ghost towns within easy reach of Socorro is Kelly, about two miles southeast of Magdalena. The town was a mining center from the mid-1800s until 1945. It produced almost $30 million in ore from mines with names such as Ambrosia, Vindicator, Hard Scrabble and the Graphic, one of the big producers of the day.

The annual cost of living in Socorro for 2.86 persons is about $8,500 per year. The county features a variety of housing in all price ranges. The average price of a three-bedroom house is $58,000. Single-family houses are available for rent or purchase. Apartments, duplexes and fourplexes are for rent either furnished or unfurnished. Two- and three-bedroom apartments rent for $400 to $500 a month; two-story townhomes, for $600. Mobile home parks are also available in and around Socorro. Mobile homes can be rented for anywhere from $90 to $100 a month or are for sale and suitable for placement on individual lots.

Four senior-retirement apartment complexes are located in town. One complex has one- and two-bedroom units ranging from $200 to $300 a month. There is a six-month waiting list. No arrangements in this complex exist for transportation, health care or activities. The apartments are Region 7 and Rental Assist Farmer's Home-supported. Another is HUD-sponsored and has one-, two- and three-bedroom units ranging from $237 to $345 a month. There is a two- to six-month wait depending on size of unit desired. Health care and transportation are provided, but there are no planned activities. The third apartment project in Socorro is also HUD supported and has one-, two- and three-bedroom units. Rentals are $250. There is a waiting list of 20 to 30 people for this complex. No transportation, health care or activities are provided. Medical expenses and income determine how rent is charged in another Socorro apartment complex for the elderly. One-bedroom units rent for $400 a month. There is no waiting list and home-health care, health-care transportation and activities are provided.

There is also a 40-unit garden apartment retirement complex in Socorro sponsored by Socorro Senior Citizen's Club, featuring individual, self-sufficient one-bedroom units with a supplemental rental feature under FHA. Rental rates depend on income. Exclusively for those 62 years and older, a 650-square-foot one-bedroom unit with patio rents for $64 to $381 a month, depending on income. Most residents are women. There have been nine vacancies in four years. While these units were constructed for low-income individuals, management reports the complex has had a difficult time filling vacancies with low-income candidates. At this writing there was a small waiting list. Transportation by daily bus to Social Security and meal sites and weekly shopping is provided. Senior companion programs and activities are offered through the senior center.

Several senior centers and meal sites serve the county. The city of Socorro has the largest, active community-oriented center. Open from 8 a.m. to 5 p.m. daily, the center serves lunch for a 75-cent donation. A senior-companion program is supported by the center. Volunteers are paid a small hourly wage and work four hours a day. The center also operates a home-assurance program that calls homebound seniors. Foster Grandparents, Senior Olympics and Meals on Wheels are also actively supported by the center. Home-health care is available through Socorro General Hospital. For further information contact Socorro City/County Senior Citizens Program, 1410 Ake St., P.O. Box 1883, Socorro, N.M. 87801; (505) 835-2119.

Several senior-interest groups meet in Socorro. AARP has an office in Socorro, as does the Retired Teachers' Association. The National Association of Retired Federal Employees is also active.

Socorro has 10 doctors, three dentists, opticians, therapists and related support groups for health-care services. The Socorro General Hospital is a 32-bed facility that opened in 1984. It features the latest medical diagnostic equipment and services, including X-ray, ICU, lab and emergency room. The hospital has full inpatient and outpatient services.

A 62-bed, longterm health care, non-profit facility has been serving Socorro since 1980. This facility features around-the-clock nursing, planned activities, a special dietary department, social services and support services. Ninety-two percent of the residents use Medicaid. The nursing home acts as an information clearinghouse for senior resources. For further information about Socorro, write the chamber of commerce at P.O. Box 743, Socorro, N.M. 87801; (505) 835-0424; www.socorro-nm.com, e-mail: chamber@socorro-nm.com.

MAGDALENA—WHERE THE OLD WEST LIVES

Twenty-seven miles west of Socorro on U.S. 60 the little town of Magdalena (population 913) lies at the foot of the mountains that bear the same name as the village. The rich history of mining and ranching has left a deep impression on this colorful little town, and ranching is still the biggest activity in the area. Increasingly, active retirees seek out Magdalena as a good place to relocate. The clean crisp mountain air and water are advantages for those who wish to settle in or around the town, but the altitude (6,500 feet) should be taken into consideration by those deciding to move here. The town now has its own clinic that is open five days a week. The Magdalena Senior Citizens Center at 202 Spruce serves the village and provides a center for retirees. You can write the center at the Spruce Street address or P.O. Box 495, Magdalena, N.M. 87825, (505) 854-2589.

The public library, staffed mainly by senior volunteers, encourages retirees to offer their services. In addition, the Area Arts and Crafts Council holds two shows a year and encourages new members. The renovated Magdalena Hall Hotel provides efficiency apartments for low-income renters.

Those who want to come to the village to see if it is a suitable relocation site can park their trailers or RVs in several locations in town for very modest fees. Single-family homes sell for $40,000-$100,000. At the low end of this range, the houses tend to be "fixer uppers" that might require renovation, and hence more money than the purchase price indicates. Retirees should be aware of figuring these extra expenditures into the purchase price, as well as the effort and additional stress of remodeling.

The entire town heats and cooks with propane. Natural gas is not available, although a favorite choice for residents is woodstove heat. While wood can be purchased already cut, still you must trim down the cut wood and carry the ashes for disposal on a daily basis during heating season. Some folks think wood heat is dirty, but others say they feel warmer than they do when heating with forced air furnaces. A good way to check out the town is to order the weekly town paper, *The Magdalena Mountain Mail*, ($35 a year for a subscription), P.O. Box 86, Magdalena, N.M. 87825. Other communities in the area also receive coverage, so one can check out the entire area. Another good way to learn about the town out is by writing the chamber of commerce, P.O. Box 281, Magdalena, N.M. 87825; (866) 854-2576; www.magdalena-nm.com.

Above—*A keen eye and little imagination reveals the shape of an elephant in the butte for which Elephant Butte State Park, New Mexico's largest body of water, was named. Photo by Arnold Vigil,* New Mexico Magazine.

TRUTH OR CONSEQUENCES—RECREATION PARADISE OF THE SOUTHWEST

Long before Truth or Consequences acquired its odd name, nomadic Indians visited the healing hot springs nearby. During cowboy days, local cowpokes built an adobe bathhouse at Paloma Springs near the Engle ferry. In the 1920s, dams created Caballo Reservoir and Elephant Butte Reservoir, named for the rock formations that rise from the water of the lake created by the dam. The town was called Hot Springs and became a resort destination when people came here to use the waters at the Geronimo Hot Springs. Although the waters are therapeutic, they do not have the usual sulfurous smell associated with most hot springs.

In 1950, Ralph Edwards, the host of the popular radio game show "Truth or Consequences," offered free publicity and an annual fiesta with Hollywood celebrities to any town that would change its name to Truth or Consequences. Citizens of Hot Springs, through a series of widely debated elections, voted to change the town's name. The town remains a friendly resort village interested in its older citizens.

Two events highlight the T or C yearly calendar. In early May, the Ralph Edwards Fiesta brings Hollywood and the New Mexico desert together. The Easter Balloon Rally fills the town with color and excitement. The nearby Hillsboro Apple Festival over Labor Day weekend is a reminder of simpler Old West days. In the fall the New Mexico State Old-Time Fiddler's Contest is nationally known for its quality and excitement.

Sierra County, with Truth or Consequences (population 7,289) as the county seat, is best known as a year-round recreation paradise. The reputation is founded on the presence of the largest lakes in New Mexico. There's more water in the county than anywhere else in the state. Elephant Butte and Caballo Lakes (48,058 surface acres, or 75 square miles) have water skiing, windsurfing, sailing, house and motor boating, parasailing and fishing. State parks at both lakes provide RV facilities, camping and picnicking. Marinas offer boat rentals, slips and mooring. Fuel, ice, food, fishing tackle, bait and boat supplies are for sale. Black, white and striper bass as well as catfish, crappie and walleye are quarry for the angler. Lodging, restaurants and boat servicing and repair are all available.

The lakes and the mineral waters of T or C have attracted seniors from all over the country to the town, located 4,260 feet above sea level. Average rainfall is only 8.5 inches yearly, and humidity is a low 10 to 15 percent. The sun shines 85 percent of the time in T or C. Average high temperatures range from a low of about 46 degrees to highs in the 74-degree range. January highs and lows are 54 degrees and 27 degrees respectively. In July, temperatures range from 92 to 66 degrees. The county has absolutely no polluting industry. The skies are brilliant blue in the day and filled with stars at night.

While much of the recreational activities in the area focus on the nearby reservoirs, two golf courses and tennis courts, a municipal swimming pool and ballparks serve local residents. The library has a large collection of Southwest material for the browser. Those interested in the hot springs can visit Geronimo Hot Springs Museum. Seven hot mineral bathhouses operate in Truth of Consequences

The Ralph Edwards Wing of the museum tells the story of the name change from Hot Springs to Truth or Consequences. The museum also features an outstanding collection of Mimbres pottery and artifacts representing American Indian cultures that lived in the area from A.D. 950 to 1250. The museum is open from 9 a.m. to 5 p.m. Monday through Saturday. A small convention center has a capacity of 4,375, and a civic and activities center serves 800 people. Bowling has been recently added to the list of T or C activities. A civic recreation center where many seniors meet their friends for dominoes, cards and shuffleboard is also popular. There are ghost towns to visit in nearby mountains. Hiking, camping and hunting are close by.

Above—A park in Truth or Consequences pays homage to the 1950s radio personality who challenged the community of Hot Springs to change its name to that of a popular game show. Photo by Mark Nohl, New Mexico Magazine.

About 400 homes come on the market annually, including resale mobile homes. Housing in the area is moderately priced in the $50,000 range. Twelve mobile home parks are in T or C, and one mobile home park is located at Caballo Lake. Three senior-housing complexes can be found in town and the same number of low-income-qualifying housing complexes. One new 87-lot senior manufactured-home complex has opened in the town. This gated facility has on-site management and the lease price (6 cents a square foot) includes water, sewer and clubhouse privileges. Each site has a covered patio, a carport, deck, shed and landscaping included in the park fee. Senior citizen and family apartments are available from the Truth or Consequences Housing Authority. Call (505) 894-2244 for information, or write T or C Housing Authority at 5 N. Cedar, T or C, N.M. 87901.

The community has its own park and a golf course nearby, and it is only one mile from lakeside. People of all ages are comfortable taking walks day or night in business districts or residential areas. Due to the town's unique location, several agencies police the locale, providing law enforcement to the town. A definite attraction for seniors who are interested in T or C is the wide assortment of people from different walks of life and from all over the world who come to settle in this beautiful part of the Southwest. The town prides itself on being friendly, open and hospitable.

Sierra Vista Hospital is a 32-bed facility with a four-bed, intensive-care unit. The hospital has general surgery, outpatient surgery and outpatient services. Helicopter service to the University of New Mexico Hospital in Albuquerque or to El Paso puts specialists within easy reach. The hospital has physicians practicing in most consulting capacities and features physical and respiratory therapy. The town is served by 12 doctors, two nurse practitioners, three dentists, two optometrists, an eye surgeon, two chiropractors and four home-health-care services.

A 110-bed nursing home recently was constructed on a hill overlooking the town to provide resident care. A veterans center on 12 landscaped acres provides full and intermediate care for resident vets from all over the country. The center has 176 beds. The Home Health Care Service in Sierra County as well as two medical clinics in town provide service to county residents. The county also has a full-service Emergency Medical Services Program.

The Retired Senior Volunteer Program in T or C is very active and a great source of information for those wanting to orient to senior services and activities in the area. There is a constant series of activities generated by the program: Senior Olympics, foster grandparents for exceptional children (offering nominal stipends, meals and mileage reimbursement and recreational activities). The Volunteer Program is a key resource for seniors in T or C. It has established an Alzheimer's group and can refer you to ongoing clubs, leisure-time activities, Alcoholics Anonymous, veterans groups, garden clubs and dancing groups. Also a great source of information and activities for seniors is the Sierra Joint Office on Aging located in the Senior Recreation Center; (505) 894-6641. For more information, write the program at 304 W. Fourth St., T or C, N.M. 87901; (505) 894-3045. Two associations for seniors are AARP and the National Association of Retired Federal Employees.

For further information on senior and other services, contact the T or C Chamber of Commerce at P.O. Drawer 31, Truth or Consequences, N.M. 87901; (505) 894-3536, (800) 831-9487; www.truthorconsequences.com, e-mail: cofc@riolink.com.

FAVORABLE CLIMATE WITHOUT SEASONAL EXTREMES

The Gila (pronounced HEE-lah) Mountain Area is known for its wild desert and mountain scenery and its excellent retirement options. Deming is the latest discovery as a retirement destination.

For more than 30 years, George Brand was an engineer operator for a number of railroads, and his wife, Esther, worked in a sweater mill. When their children left their Quakertown, Pa., home in 1975, the Brands began an odyssey all over the country during which they thought of relocating to the various places they visited. Nothing seemed quite suited to their needs. Then, in 1978, they were driving to Arizona with another couple when they stopped for gas in Deming. They stayed the night and were captivated by the town.

The following year they vacationed in Deming and knew that this was where they wanted to retire. Now they are avid members of the Deming Gem and Mineral Society. George loves working in his shop while Esther takes pride in her cactus garden.

"The people here in Deming are so nice and friendly," Esther says. "And the lack of humidity really helped my arthritis."

Other towns in the Gila Mountain Area await discovery as well. The locale is rich in climate and recreational resources. If you are a rockhound, this is paradise. Health resources have taken a turn for the better as

Right—Resembling Europe's famous and mysterious Stonehenge, the volcanic formations at City of Rocks State Park near Deming tantalize the imagination. Photo by Mark Nohl, New Mexico Magazine.

people in the area wake up to the potential their communities represent to retirees who are looking for beautiful places to live with clean air and a reasonable cost of living.

DEMING—KINGDOM OF THE SUN

About half of Deming's 14,116 citizens are retirees. The town actively promotes its many advantages for seniors. Deming has produced its own video that features attractions to be found in the area for retirees. You can order the VHS tape for $8 plus $3 shipping by writing the Deming/Luna County Chamber of Commerce, 800 E. Pine, Deming, N.M. 88031; (505) 546-2674, (800) 848-4955. The 26-minute tape covers retirement attractions and takes you on three tours originating from town. Also, visit the Deming Web site at www.demingchamber.com, or e-mail: chamber@zianet.com.

One tour leaves Deming and travels south to Rock Hound State Park. As the name suggests, this park, covering 250 acres on the western slopes of the rugged Florida Mountains, is littered with minerals and you don't have to be an expert to enjoy picking up attractive stones. There are also semi-precious stones and gem rocks there for the picking. You can spend hours enjoying the rocks and then camp or picnic, sampling the beauty of this rockhounder's paradise. The tour leads to Columbus through Spring Canyon Park. Columbus is the little town Pancho Villa raided in 1916 and Pancho Villa State Park is nearby.

The town of Columbus (population 1,765) promotes mobile home and con-

ventional homesites to retirees through the Development Board. Raw land in 20-
to 160-acre tracts sells for $150 to $600 per acre. A 100-foot by 140-foot
homesite sells for $3,000. Taxes on these lots are $10 a year. At 4,080 feet,
the town possesses a clear, dry climate with summer-mean temperatures of
77.3 degrees and winter-mean temperatures of 47.5 degrees. Annual precipitation is 8 inches and the sun shines 335 days a year. Relative humidity is 20
to 25 percent. Lots are available for trailers, motor homes, mobile homes and
conventional houses. Municipal water connections are about $245 and septic
systems cost $800. Raw land in 20- to 160-acre tracts sells for $150 to $600
an acre depending on location, access and utility availability. Contact the
Columbus Chamber, Box 365, Columbus, N.M. 88029. For further information, call (505) 531-2479.

From Columbus, motorists can take an excursion to Las Palomas in
Chihuahua, Mexico, and then back to Deming. The tour takes at least a half-
day and is about 110 miles round trip.

Another tour takes you north of Deming to Nutt, Lake Valley and Hillsboro
and then on to City of Rocks State Park. This park might remind you of
Stonehenge or the skyline of a mysterious city of stone covering one square
mile. Picnic sites and a camping area are featured. On the last leg of the tour
back to Deming, visitors can bathe in the healing mineral waters at Faywood
Hot Springs.

A final tour also heads north of town and goes to the Santa Rita open-pit
copper mine, which covers four square miles and is 1,000 feet deep. The route
travels along the crest of the Gila Mountains and then down into the valley
along the Gila River. Stop at the Gila Cliff Dwellings inhabited by the Mogollón
Indians from A.D. 1280 to the early 1300s. The tour returns to Deming through
Pinos Altos, an old ghost town, partially restored, that has a museum and an
opera house.

Deming's climate has much to offer retired citizens who want to relocate.
Average rainfall is about 9 inches per year. Snow occasionally falls in winter
and disappears instantly. At 4,331 feet, summer days get up to the 90s and
cool to the 50s. In winter, skies are crisp and blue and temperatures climb to
the 50s. Humidity is low, sometimes only 5 percent, and the air is clean.

At one time retired folks used to go to Phoenix for clean, dry air. Now
they're looking at moving to places like Deming. Lung patients will also find the

town's warm weather a great benefit. Clean water is a plus—the town advertises the water as 99.9 percent pure.

The Santa Fe and Southern Pacific railroads meet in Deming, and the town is served by U.S. 180 and Interstate 10. Intercity bus companies stop in Deming, and the local airport has a 6,619-foot runway.

The town is known for its wacky Great American Duck Race, a twice-annual affair conducted the fourth week in August and the third weekend in February. The duck races have been featured on national television and have received international press coverage. The chamber of commerce's self-humorous promotion for the town declares Deming home of "pure water and fast ducks."

The Río Mimbres Country Club has an 18-hole course open all year and a swimming pool, dining room, bar, racquetball courts and planned member activities. The town also has two pools, tennis courts, a bowling alley and a winery. The Deming Luna Mimbres Museum is also an interesting attraction housed in the old armory building. Samples of the incredibly beautiful Mimbres Indian pottery are exhibited. There is a room with more than 600 dolls displayed, a quilt room, a Western tack room and exhibits of Southwestern life of the past.

The Community Concert Association and Deming Arts Council stimulate local cultural life and bring artists of national prominence to town. The town's Center for the Arts has a 500-seat auditorium for performances and concerts. The 50,000-volume library is noted for its fine Southwestern history collection. Lectures, exhibits and special presentations are often featured at the library.

The Deming Senior Citizens Center is a lively and well-supported focus of life for retired people in Deming. The center sponsors a spring Senior Olympics, regular dances and events, arts and crafts and a host of volunteer programs. More than 80 civic groups are active in Deming. Write the Senior Center at 720 S. Granite, Deming, N.M. 88030, or call (505) 546-8823 for more information.

Retired people find cost of living an extremely important factor in determining where they choose to live. In 1989 Rand McNally ranked Deming fourth in the nation in terms of retirement cities for cost of housing. The survey of 131 cities put median housing costs in Deming at $38,800. Now (year 2001) median housing costs have only gone up to $45,000. The town also ranked

Above—The biannual Deming Duck Race has grown from a local promotional event to a much-anticipated regional extravaganza that delights both young and old. Photo by Mark Nohl, New Mexico Magazine.

third in terms of property tax rates. The average price for a three-bedroom house in town is $68,000. Property taxes for a two-bedroom, one-and-one-half bath, 1,200-square-foot house worth $49,500 would run about $235 a year. One-bedroom, furnished apartments rent for $275 with gas paid. A one-bedroom, unfurnished apartment rents for $260 with gas also paid. A two-bedroom furnished rents for $280 to $310; unfurnished, from $260 to $290.

Raw land around town is marketed for as little as $250 an acre, but building lots in the "ranchette area" sell for more like $8,000 an acre. This 120-acre area has sites suitable for standard-home development and mobile homes. Deming also had the sixth highest percentage of mobile homes of the communities surveyed. A 144-acre subdivision features mobile home and townhouse sites near the golf course. Ten percent of the sites are suitable for public use. Three other subdivisions are also under construction in the Deming area.

There are two mobile home parks in and near Deming. One in town features a clubhouse for residents. Proximity to shopping, security lighting, fencing, underground utilities with cable television, landscaping and paved driveways, laundry facilities, bingo, shuffleboard and planned potlucks are some of the features for residents. RV parks are common, and one development, five minutes from downtown, allows both mobile homes and single-family houses. The park encourages an active community life.

The retirement-living complex most prominent in Deming offers 102 studio, one- and two-bedroom apartments with maintenance and utilities provided. Forty-six of these units operate under HUD Section 8 housing regulations. This government-housing subsidy means an applicant must meet low-income standards and pay 30 percent of adjusted income. Fifty-six units in the complex operate under HUD Section 202 guidelines. An occupant must either be disabled or at least 62 years old. In addition, there are geographic income standards that a tenant must meet. Again, an occupant must pay 30 percent of adjusted gross income for rent. These apartments have fixed rents. Utilities are included in rental fees for one- and two-bedroom units. The center is located near the hospital and has recreational facilities and scheduled activities. There is a headquarters/clubhouse, recreation hall and library. The dining hall operates on a potluck basis. A lapidary shop, woodworking shop and shuffleboard and horseshoe areas provide residents recreational opportunities. Two coin-operated laundries are available. Turnover at the facility is low.

Health care in Luna County has undergone dramatic improvements. Twenty-one physicians and seven dentists serve the town. Mimbres Memorial Hospital has undergone a 12,000-foot expansion and now has 60 patient beds. A new emergency room, expanded lab facility and X-ray facilities have been added as well as respiratory therapy and operating and recovery rooms. The $2.7 million expansion emphasizes outpatient services with more bed space for cardiac and intensive care. New doctors' offices have been completed, and there is an excellent ambulance service. Adjoining the hospital is a 70-bed nursing home.

LORDSBURG—OLD WEST COUNTRY

Tucked away at 4,145 feet in the Pyramid Valley in the bootheel of southwestern New Mexico is Lordsburg, a town of 3,379 inhabitants. The population remains rather young here. Despite the size of the community and the draw of larger urban areas, many young people who have grown up in Lordsburg choose to stay in the community.

The major employer is Phelps-Dodge, which operates a copper smelter near town. New thermally heated greenhouses, a premanufactured-housing plant and a budding wine industry also support the town's economy.

The climate in Lordsburg is an attraction for retirees. The average January high temperature is 55 degrees, with lows of 26 degrees. In July, highs reach 95 and lows are in the mid-60s. Snowfall is almost 5 inches in January but does not stay on the ground for more than a few hours. In July, rains of 2 inches are recorded. Low humidity and ample sunshine make this climate ideal for those who suffer respiratory difficulties. Year-round sunshine and spectacular desert and mountain scenery characterize the area.

Above—*An abandoned ranching homestead reminds of the past on the edge of the Gila National Forest in the Silver City area, where many mining towns went boom then bust. Photo by Mark Nohl,* New Mexico Magazine.

The town has a library, movie theater and four parks. There are 23 civic clubs. Highways (I-10), Greyhound and AMTRAK service connect Lordsburg with the outside world; there also is a municipal airport.

Both Gila National Forest and Coronado National Forest offer recreational opportunities. North of town, the Red Rock area and the Gila River bottom are wild and beautiful. Hunting is big in Hidalgo County. Javelina, the wild desert boar, bighorn sheep and game birds are the quarry. The Hatchet Mountains are as rugged as they sound, and the Lower Gila River provides fishing excitement all year for those who want to catch catfish, trout and smallmouth bass. Rockhounds love the surrounding country, a veritable playground for those who like to hunt gemstones. There are many abandoned mines in the area. The Coronado Forest also offers volcanic glass and Gold Gulch, which still has opportunities for the amateur prospector.

Shakespeare and Steins are two nearby ghost towns. The graveyard in Shakespeare is an interesting reminder of those days of past glory when mineral wealth and greed drew folks from all over to mine until the 1893 depression wiped out the town.

Low taxes and affordable housing are touted as advantages for retired people who want to settle in Lordsburg. The average price of a new three-bedroom house is $34,000. Modular homes manufactured locally cost $30 per square foot and come carpeted, with stove and dishwasher furnished. Raw land in town is priced at less than $4,000 a lot. One-bedroom apartments rent for as little as $200 unfurnished. Two-bedroom furnished apartments rent for $290.

For a town of its size, Lordsburg offers a good deal of support to senior citizens The town has an excellent nursing home with 60 beds that has an assisted-living program and a clinic with four part-time physicians. For more extensive health-care needs, Silver City's Gila Regional Medical Center provides full-service specialty care. Two home-help agencies and a fine rural ambulance service are a draw for retirees who seek medical support. Crime rates are also low.

The Lordsburg-Hidalgo County Senior Citizens Program, 317 E. Fourth St., Lordsburg, N.M. 88045, is the center of senior life in town; (505) 542-9414. Lunch is provided five days a week and delivered to the homebound. The program offers transportation to and from the center and for shopping and medical appointments. Transportation out of the Lordsburg area is provided once a month. Daily recreation, arts and crafts, exercise, games, birthday parties, picnics, potlucks and blood-pressure checks are conducted at the center. A seniors' referral-and-information service and a homemaker service operate out of the center.

For information about Lordsburg, write the chamber of commerce, 117 E. Second St., Lordsburg, N.M. 88045-1927; (505) 542-9864; www.gilanet.com/lordsburgcoc, e-mail: lordsburgcoc@gilanet.com.

SILVER CITY—CLIMATE CAPITAL AND RETIREMENT DESTINATION

Silver City, at an altitude of 6,000 feet, boasts the best median, annual temperature of any location in the country. The average temperature in January is 49 on the high side and 24 on the low side. The sun shines 83.3 percent of the time. On only about two days during winter will temperatures go below freezing. Snow falls but seldom causes any disruption. In July, temperatures go from 59 degrees to 83.4 degrees. The normal growing season is 179 days a year, with relative humidity 31 percent and precipitation 16.85 inches. Nights in summer are cool and the wind prevails at 10 mph out of the west to north-west.

Retirees are discovering Silver City (population 10,545) because of the moderate climate and the cost of living. One retiree even says he prefers Silver City to Hawaii. Architecturally, Silver City is blessed and the National Trust for Historic Preservation chose it to participate in the Main Street Project to bring improvements to the downtown area.

The Silver City Museum occupies the H.B. Ailman House. Constructed in 1881, the house is listed on the National Register of Historic Places. Various facets of life, including Victoriana on the frontier, are featured. Silver City has four nationally recognized historic districts. Self-guided walking tours can be followed using guides purchased for 25 cents at the chamber of commerce or the Silver City Museum. At the turn of the century, a series of floods wiped out Main Street buildings constructed during the 1870s and 1880s. The result is the unusual Big Ditch Park that creates a pleasant downtown oasis.

At Western New Mexico University, the museum housed in Fleming Hall features an outstanding exhibit of Mimbres pottery. Other Southwestern collections focus on 19th-century life. Fleming Hall is one of the most prominent and oldest buildings on campus. The town is also where Billy the Kid grew up, and you can read about his early years before he became the famous outlaw renegade.

The outdoors offer a variety of activities in and around Silver City. Bird watchers have a field day, spotting the great blue heron, Mexican jay, Montezuma quail and dozens of other species that pass through or reside in the region.

Rockhounding is a favorite pastime. Copper is especially abundant and the alert mineral hunter can find turquoise, moon stone, meerschaum, petrified wood and limonite. Rockhounds can also pan for gold in streams near Silver City.

Hiking, backpacking and tenting in the 3.3 million-acre Gila Wilderness offer a wonderful experience. There are many lakes around Silver City where trout enthusiasts can venture: Lake Roberts, Quemado Lake, Snow Lake, Bill Evans Lake and several others offer amusement and challenges. For those who like open, moving water, the Tularosa River and San Francisco River Box as

Above—*The Territorial architecture of the Silver City Museum is a prime example of this southwestern town's deep historical link to the past. Photo by Mark Nohl,* New Mexico Magazine.

well as several creeks offer a test for the avid fly-fisherman or the bait fisherman.

One of the most popular scenic drives encompasses a 75-mile loop from Silver City to Santa Rita, site of a huge open-pit copper mine up the beautiful Mimbres Valley. If you are in the valley on the weekend of Memorial Day, be sure to see the Mimbres Sawdust Festival. National championship chainsaw artist Jerry Ward carves figures from native logs. Arts and crafts booths, country fiddle music, a barbecue and a logging contest all take place on an aromatic carpet of sawdust under a grove of black walnut and juniper trees. Spend time at a dude ranch in the valley for a more extended stay. From the Mimbres Valley, the drive heads down Sapillo Creek and across the Pinos Altos Mountains back to Silver City. For those in shape, this tour can be done by bike.

Forty-four miles north of town on the edge of the Gila Wilderness is Gila Cliff Dwellings National Monument: Indian ruins of some 40 rooms invite exploration. Also, 68 miles north of town you can experience the Catwalk, a 250-foot metal walkway that clings to the sides of the boulder-choked Whitewater Canyon. In some places the canyon is only 20-feet wide and

Above—*The Gila Wilderness was the first designated wilderness area in the nation, its natural rugged beauty guaranteed by law to be protected from future development. Photo by Mark Nohl,* New Mexico Magazine.

250-feet deep. If you want to explore an old mining town, go to Mogollón, 3.5 miles north of Glenwood off a steep, winding mountain road. The City of Rocks formation can also be reached from Silver City. Several hot springs can be found near town. Local residents are pleased to give directions. For those who travel by RV, there are a number of facilities in town.

Many recreational opportunities exist in Silver City, including three swimming pools, 10 parks, an 18-hole golf course and a country club. The town's library has a collection of 35,000 volumes. Fiction, non-fiction and reference books on the Southwest and New Mexico as well as a local-history collection, a genealogy collection of more than 300 books and a talking-book service are some of the features. Western New Mexico University offers a pleasant, small campus that provides educational focus for the town.

The nearest international airport can be found 156 miles to the south in El Paso, Texas, but Silver City is served by Mesa Airlines. U.S. 80 as well as state highways provide highway access.

Silver City actively promotes itself as a retirement location and has established Silver City/Grant County Economic Development Corporation (SIGRED).

The area offers good health care. The Gila Regional Medical Center is an 88-bed general hospital staffed by 32 physicians in all specialty areas. There is an intensive coronary-care unit equipped with the latest monitoring devices, a cardiac-rehab unit and cardiac-care unit. X-ray facilities include nuclear medicine and stress testing. Hospital Social Service offers home-health and hospice needs. The Fort Bayard Medical Center, a state-operated, 213-bed facility, provides longterm care for the elderly. It has an exceptional drug- and alcohol-treatment program as well as outpatient services, physical therapy and rehab services. More than 160 professionals are on staff, with three physicians.

The Community Health Department offers immunization, community health and nutrition clinics and many other services. An intermediate-care facility, which is federally certified and state licensed, provides nursing care for residents under an individual-care plan monitored and changed periodically to promote as much independence as possible and still meet residents' needs. Beauty, barber and physical-therapy services are also available. The facility employs a staff of up to 40. There are also three rest homes in town with 120 beds. There is a retirement-condominium project in town on East Pine Street. Thirty-one doctors and 10 dentists serve Silver City and the surrounding area. There is good emergency ground and air transport.

A number of retirement organizations flourish in town. Among them are veterans groups, the golf association, retired teachers and retired volunteers. Single-family homes start as low as $25,000 and go up to the $100,000 range. Cabins, homes, ranches and farms are available at reasonable prices.

There are two key contacts in Silver City for those interested in the senior life in town. The Area Council for Services to Senior Citizens and the Silver City Senior Center are both at 811 D St., P.O. Box 2472, Silver City, N.M. 88041; (505) 388-2544. The Silver City Chamber of Commerce takes pleasure in showing visitors and prospective residents what the community has to offer. For further information, write the chamber at 201 N. Hudson St., Silver City, N.M. 88061; (505) 538-3785, (800) 548-9378; www.silvercity.org, e-mail: sgcchamber@cybermesa.com.

A RETIREMENT BOUNTY-EXCELLENT CLIMATE AT RELATIVELY LOW ALTITUDES

Sun Country, encompassing New Mexico's southeastern quadrant, spans an incredibly broad spectrum of opportunities for retirees. One of New Mexico's most celebrated retirement destinations, Roswell, awaits discovery here. But there is every variety of retired living available in this region of sun, desert and mountain.

"You want it in one word?" asks retired oil worker Glenn Howard about what drew him to Artesia. "Climate! It's not too severe, either, in winter or summer." Howard, who hails from north-central Texas, also credits the Southwestern tradition of hospitality as an attraction as well as the variety of activities for seniors. A confirmed and active member of the AARP Artesia chapter, Howard enjoys visiting senior centers, not just in his town but wherever he travels with his wife. They love roving the countryside, following a gypsy life, in their travel trailer. When they get back to Artesia, Howard follows his passion for being a ham-radio operator. The Howards also like to spend time in the garden; whenever the urge strikes, they go fishing in some of their favorite local spots.

From the beautiful mountain resort town of Ruidoso to the towns that border Texas, retirees are finding hidden gems as well as more obvious locations, discovering the keys that unlock the many charms of Sun

Above—*Nearly every night in every corner of New Mexico, a magnificent display of colors paint the expansive skies like this sunset just north of Artesia. Photo by Arnold Vigil,* New Mexico Magazine.

Country for easy and luxurious retired living.

ALAMOGORDO—HEART OF THE TULAROSA BASIN

Alamogordo (population 35,582) is on the east side of the Tularosa Basin, one of the largest undrained basins in the world. The basin is bordered on the west by the San Andres Mountains and the 8,000-foot Organ Mountains, and on the east by the 9,000-foot Sacramento Mountains. An ancient sea once occupied the more than 4,000-square-mile basin, and a remnant of this ocean remains in a subsurface reservoir of salt water that underlies it. The Tularosa Basin is also site of White Sands National Monument, a 2,220-square-mile white gypsum desert 14 miles south of Alamogordo.

The mountain ranges on either side of the basin account for mild climatic conditions prevailing in Alamogordo, which sits at elevation of 4,350 feet. In January, the coldest month, the mean monthly high is 54 degrees and the low is 30. In summer, the average high is 95 and the low is 60. There are about 213 frost-free days a year, and the sun shines about 75 percent of the time. The visitor can drive 16 miles east of Alamogordo to Cloudcroft and experience conditions remarkably like the Canadian Rockies, with only 136 frost-free days and brisk alpine conditions.

Rainfall in the basin averages about 10 inches a year. In the nearby mountains it can rain from 15 to 48 inches a year. The rainiest period in the basin is from June through August. Breathtaking thunderstorms that suddenly break in large thunderheads roll through the afternoon sky, leaving cool, fair conditions after they pass. In winter, occasional snows quickly disappear from the ground. The uplift of the Sacramento Mountains and concurrent settling of the basin has exposed an accumulated rock record of 500 million years of geologic history exposed along the western edge of the Sacramentos. Here, amateur geologists can discover fossils and examine this fascinating reminder of our planet's past. Due to the wide variation in climatic conditions in the area, the plants and animals are as varied as the geology, which ranges from desert to mountain crest with all ecological zones between these two extremes. Mesquite, creosote and many varieties of cactus line the valley floor. At higher elevations piñon and juniper give way to pine and fir, and above timberline, alpine meadows prevail. From lofty summits, views stretch 100 miles.

Alamogordo's modern history began when Charles B. and John Eddy, early promoters, first dreamed of a city growing at the site of present-day Alamogordo. The area is alive with the history of the Mescalero Apache wars. Near Alamogordo Geronimo led his unsuccessful insurrection against the U.S. Cavalry. During the Lincoln County War, Blazer's Mill was the site of a bloody battle. The history of the Southwest is in the soil, the rocks and air of this country. It offers countless hours of fascinating exploration for those who choose to settle in this intriguing land.

Alamogordo's history took a new course when Holloman Air Base was constructed during World War II and the first atomic bomb was detonated to the northwest at Trinity Site toward the end of the war. With these events and the development of nearby White Sands Missile Range, Alamogordo stepped from being a sleepy little desert town into the Space Age. For the next 15 or so years members of the German Air Force will be training at the base, adding a tremendous boost to the local economy.

On the outskirts of Alamogordo, a golden structure gleams against a hillside. This is the four-story International Space Hall of Fame, housing one of the finest collections of space memorabilia in the world. Next door to the hall is the Clyde W. Tombaugh Space Theater, one of the few Omnimax® theaters in the country. Here the viewer is wrapped in sound and surrounded by images emanating from one of the largest screens you will ever see, offering incredibly high resolution. Combination tickets for both attractions are available. Many people have discovered that Alamogordo has just what they want in a retirement location. The city has become a major retirement town since the early 1980s when *Modern Maturity* published the results of the Chase Econometrics study of the most favorable retirement locations in the country. The study ranked New Mexico one of the top-10 states for desirable retirement location, ahead of Arizona, Colorado and Florida.

The Alameda Park Zoo, established in 1898, is the oldest zoo in the Southwest, boasting more than 260 animals on exhibit. Near the park, the Tularosa Basin Historical Society operates a museum that features historic photographs of the area. The museum is next door to the chamber of commerce.

Alamogordo is well-served by highways and road systems. Commercial-air service is available at the Alamogordo-White Sands Regional Airport. As a retirement destination, Alamogordo definitely has appeal. There is a Civic Center in town with kitchen facilities that can seat 450. Alamogordo has 15 public parks, a golf course, two swimming pools, 12 tennis courts, baseball and soccer fields, and racquetball courts. New Mexico State University at Alamogordo is a two-year school. The Alamogordo Community Education Program also offers many educational opportunities to citizens in a relaxed and informal setting. Classes are offered five times a year. Information on educational opportunities in the community is provided by the chamber of commerce.

The housing market offers a variety of homes in several styles. Older homes are adobe or Victorian style, while many of the more recent houses are constructed in single-story Ranch style. Most of these homes are priced in the $50,000-$90,000 range. Generally, older homes go for less money. There are several large apartment complexes in town and many duplex and fourplex units. Buying these units, living in one and renting others can be a possibility for retirees. A two-bedroom apartment rents for about $400 a month, while a three-bedroom unit rents for around $600 a month. The town also has an independent-living retirement community of active seniors 62 years and over. Annual-income qualifications are at least $15,000, although

Above—*Although the free-flowing lines of White Sands National Monument near Alamogordo make this a favorite spot for artists, the area also presents many opportunities for families. Photo by Mark Nohl,* New Mexico Magazine.

the complex takes into consideration other assets to determine if retirees are eligible. The community features 24-hour-entrance security, nurse-call systems in baths and bedrooms, a community room for group activities and barrier-free construction (no steps). An entrance fee is required before move-in. The fee for a one-bedroom (794 square feet) apartment is $23,840 with a monthly rent of $866. Rebates are available upon resale. There is a 48-unit, second-phase construction in the works as of this writing (2001). The town also has an assisted-living complex that offers both short-term and longterm care, nursing service and three meals a day. The town also supports two nursing homes.

Mobile homes are available for rent, with prices from $200 to $500 a month depending on size, location and amenities. There is also a manufactured-home community in Alamogordo for those 55 years and older. The community is a fully secured, walled and gated complex with more than 170 lots available for purchase, a clubhouse, heated pool and therapy spa. Single-family houses are also for rent.

Many retired citizens of Alamogordo came here originally to serve at Holloman Air Force Base, which is a complete city in itself, housing 4,000 resident-service people. White Sands Missile Range also has contributed to the retirement-age population in Alamogordo. Those in federal service who have chosen to retire to Alamogordo have done so due to good senior infrastructure in the town. Congress has announced the construction of a new VA medical center for Alamagordo, which is slated to begin operation in the latter part of 2001.

There are 50 physicians in Alamogordo and 14 dentists. Two nursing homes have a total of 210 beds. The intermediate- and skilled-care nursing facility has 120 beds in semiprivate rooms and charges daily rates. The Gerald Champion Memorial Hospital is a 91-bed general and acute-care facility with a range of medical specialties. The hospital is a certified Medicare-Medicaid provider with a fully accredited lab and 24-hour emergency service.

The focus of senior life for Alamogordo is the city- and county-supported Older American Center. The center provides 300 noontime meals and Meals on Wheels to 100 seniors daily; 350 volunteers support this effort. Sports and recreational activities are encouraged by the city, which offers a Senior Olympics program and a full range of assistance to those needing special help. Blood-pressure checks, flu immunizations and utilities assistance are also programs having full support from the community. At the New Mexico School for the Handicapped, a Foster Grandparents program brings together older citizens and young students. There are many other senior volunteer programs to take advantage of the skills and experience of retired citizens. Contact the Older Americans Center, 511 10th St., Alamogordo, N.M. 88310; (505) 434-1330. In 1995 the town completed construction on a $3 million, 22,000-square-foot senior center at 2201 Puerto Rico.

Alamogordo prides itself on its low crime rate. The town uses the Canadian public-safety system in which police officers respond to fire calls, becoming firefighters on the scene. This cost-effective system provides a high level of police and low level of fire department personnel to the town.

One of the most amazing sights of the area is White Sands National Monument. Gypsum sand dunes tower to 30 feet and extend more than 230 square miles. A 16-mile drive takes you among the dunes. While there is no camping in the area, picnicking is available. There is a car admission fee. Call (505) 437-1058 for more information.

The Oliver Lee Memorial State Park is a 180-acre overnight camping facility and the site of Dog Canyon, a steep defile with a stream that has created a miniature oasis of rock formations and plant life. Apaches found the canyon an ideal location for ambushes, and the site reverberates with the history of battles and skirmishes fought long ago. Call (505) 437-8284 for more information.

On the south side of Alamogordo, Alamo Canyon is a wonderful place to hike, hunt fossils, ride horseback or camp. About six miles north of Alamogordo visit the historic town of La Luz (population 2,000) at the mouth of La Luz Canyon. Many artists live in the area. Fresh fruits and vegetables are available in season. Up La Luz Canyon you can go the back way to Cloudcroft. The road is unpaved for the most part so you might prefer the direct way up U.S. 82.

Cloudcroft is a charming mountain town that borders Lincoln National Forest, which occupies one million acres of the Sacramento Mountains. This center for arts and crafts is also the site of many summer homes. Many people choose to retire in Alamogordo and have second homes in Cloudcroft for the pleasant, cool mountain temperatures that prevail in summer. Near the Lodge at Cloudcroft, you can play golf at one of the finest mountain courses in the country. The Sacramento Mountain Museum on the east side of town presents a fascinating look at the early days in Cloudcroft.

Closer to Alamogordo you can discover Indian sites such as Three Rivers Petroglyph National Recreation Site, located west of the Sierra Blanca Mountains. There are more than 5,000 petroglyphs across the road from ancient Indian dwellings.

One of the most rugged areas of the basin, Valley of Fires Recreation Area, features an ancient lava flow covering a 44-mile area, five miles wide. Camping and picnicking are available in the area as well as trail walking and hiking. Just to the east of Valley of Fires, visit Carrizozo (population 1,036), a small community in the foothills of the Sacramento Mountains. The town boasts moderate priced single-family homes that make the small village one of the more attractive housing markets in the area. Income-based, subsidized senior housing is available at a local apartment complex that is owned and operated by the Carrizozo Women's Club. Here you will find a nine-hole golf course at a recreation park that also features a large clubhouse and a ballroom for gatherings and dances. The town provides residents a recreational center with bowling alley, pingpong and pool tables, and a spacious community room. Carrizozo also has a swimming pool, open from mid-May to mid-September. The town has the Zia Senior Center, Box 519, Carrizozo, N.M., where senior friends gather, share a meal and participate in information exchanges and other services; (505) 648-2121. Contact the chamber or visitor center at Carrizozo, P.O. Box 567, Carrizozo, N.M. 88301; (505) 648-2732; www.townofcarrizozo.bizland.com, e-mail: zozocc@tularosa.net.

Nestled between the Capitán and Sacramento mountains at 6,300 feet, the village of Capitán (population 1,443) attracts active seniors who enjoy small-town mountain living. Birthplace and now final resting place of Smokey Bear, Capitán offers big-game hunting, fishing and skiing at nearby Ski Apache. Every Fourth of July the Smokey Bear Stampede features a rodeo, barbecue and Western dance. While the Lincoln County Medical Center is 20 miles away in Ruidoso, Capitán is served by its own EMT service. The Zia Senior Center also serves the town as an active focus for senior social life in the community. There is van transportation for shopping and medical purposes for seniors. There are a few low-income HUD qualified apartments in town for seniors, but single-family housing dominates the market. Village-owned water is scarce, however. For further information, contact the chamber of commerce, P.O. Box 441, Capitán, N.M. 88316-0441; (505) 354-2273.

The Salinas Pueblos National Monument is the site of three large pueblos called Gran Quivira, Abó and Quarai. Spanish missions were established there in the late 1600s. The ruins take one back into time. The visitor center and museum can give information about the ruins and the life led in this center of Indian civilization.

The Alamogordo Chamber of Commerce, 1301 N. White Sands Blvd., Alamogordo, N.M. 88310, offers information on retirement living in the town, facilities of interest, touring and vacation spots, various brochures on specific locations, activities and programs; call (505) 437-6120 or (800) 826-0294; reach them on the town's Web site at www.alamogordo.com, e-mail: chamber@alamogordo.com.

ARTESIA—NEW MEXICO CROSSROADS

As you might guess, Artesia (population 10,692) is named for the artesian water found in the town. The small city has been known for its central location at the crossroads of U.S. 285 and U.S. 82. The town has been very active in extractive industries and prides itself on keeping its small-town atmosphere while still providing major conveniences and fine shopping facilities.

At an elevation of 3,380 feet, Artesia enjoys year-round sunshine in a warm, semiarid climate with low humidity. Average temperatures in summer are around 80 degrees. In winter, it is mild with temperatures in the mid-40s. Annual precipitation is just more than 10 inches. The proximity of recreation and sightseeing destinations makes the town a tourist gateway city. It is within easy driving distance of White Sands National Monument, Carlsbad Caverns National Park, Bottomless Lakes State Park and the Sacramento Mountains. There is a municipal airport and intercity bus service.

The citizens of Artesia take pride in investing in their community. The city has spent more than $25 million on facilities and improvements in the past few years. Part of that investment went toward developing a new senior-citizen's center, a community center and the development of more than 350 acres of city parks.

Seven apartment complexes offer units in Artesia and there are three low-income apartment projects. One provides housing for seniors only. Artesia also has one nursing center with 80 beds and 10 apartments. There are seven doctors, seven optometrists, three chiropractic physicians, three dentists and a medical lab to serve the town.

Artesia General Hospital is a complete-care facility with 38 beds that provides swing-bed service for nursing-home care. There are nine doctors and two dentists on staff. A general surgeon who specializes in trauma care also works at the hospital. The hospital will offer diagnostic and lab services for a new Veterans Administration satellite clinic to be located in Artesia. The clinic will operate in conjunction with the VA Medical Center in Albuquerque and provide outpatient services. Eleven doctors and six dentists provide service to Artesia.

The Senior Citizens Center, 110 N. Fifth, P.O. Box 518, Artesia, N.M. 88210, (505) 748-1207, provides seniors with many activities: ceramics, dance lessons, pool lessons, lapidary courses, exercise classes, bridge and other games, tax clinics, AARP meetings, volunteer activities, meal service, fishing trips and birthday celebrations. Run by the local Commission on Aging, the center focuses on senior life in Artesia.

***Above**—Clouds, crisp light and expansive vistas and skies are a fringe benefit of the Artesia area, whose economy is fueled by oil and gas production as well as farming and ranching. Photo by Arnold Vigil, New Mexico Magazine.*

The town is adding a law-enforcement academy that will be located at the site of the former Christian College. The city of Artesia believes in its future and is known for its upbeat optimistic atmosphere. For further information contact the chamber of commerce, P.O. Box 99, Artesia, N.M. 88211; (505) 746-2744, (800) 658-6251; www.artesiachamber.com, e-mail: commerce@pvtnetworks.net.

CARLSBAD—RETIREMENT DREAM

Carlsbad (population 25,625) is the kind of place many people dream about when they think of retiring. With the Pecos River flowing through town, a great climate, plenty of recreational opportunities and senior resources, Carlsbad fulfills retirement visions.

At 3,110 feet, the city is most famous for Carlsbad Caverns National Park, a half-hour from town. The caverns open a fantastic world of caves, offering the visitor an unmatched subterranean experience. The caverns feature a snack bar and an elevator in case you get tired. The formations are all fully lit and paths are well-constructed and easy to walk. Self-guided tours take you through this amazing world beneath the surface of the earth.

The caverns are just the beginning for those who want to retire to a town that offers so much. The Lake Carlsbad Recreation Area in the heart of the city brings the pleasures of aquatic activities right to the center of town. The George Washington Steamboat tours the Pecos River past beautiful homes along the banks. Just outside of town the Living Desert State Park exhibits the plant and animal wonders of the desert with more than 100 species. The Discover Carlsbad Tour reveals city overlooks, golf courses, homes and the wandering Pecos River, the territorial square and municipal library and museum.

Climatic conditions in Carlsbad are semiarid, with mild winters and warm summers. There are 220 days between frosts and the sun shines 74 percent of the time. Average rainfall is about 12.43 inches a year, with most of this moisture falling from May through October. From mid-May to mid-September, highs are in the 90s; nighttime cooling makes the evenings pleasant and comfortable. In January, the average daytime shade temperature is near 58 degrees. It is rare if the thermometer reaches freezing until after dark. Rarely will it fall below the zero mark.

Carlsbad features a wide variety of recreational facilities and cultural opportunities, including public tennis (14 courts), two golf courses, fishing and water skiing, and an arts council that brings performing- and visual-arts attractions to town. Fees for golfing are very reasonable: for $135 one can golf for the year.

Housing is abundant and moderately priced for both rental and purchase. Apartment and home rentals range from $200 to $1,000 a month. Many homes are priced from $35,000 to $200,000 and are available throughout the city and in rural areas outside of town. Taxes on a three-bedroom house valued at $60,000 are $250 a year.

A 144-bed general hospital, Guadalupe Medical Center, offers intensive and coronary units, stress and EEG testing, physical therapy, lab services, X-ray, diagnostics, isotope scanning, pulmonary-function testing, 24-hour physician coverage in the emergency unit and many other services. More than 40 doctors provide service to Carlsbad.

Two full-service retirement communities flourish in Carlsbad. A community affiliated with a denomination serves 90 retiree residents and 220 who need nursing care. Admission is not based on ability to pay. Apartments with a 120-bed nursing center attached comprise the facilities, which offer an activities center and chapel with park frontage on the Pecos River. Housekeeping services, cafeteria-style dining, planned social and recreational activities and daily transportation are featured. Two-bedroom custom homes are also available with 24-hour emergency-call systems, low monthly service fees and a refund plan.

Also situated on the banks of the Pecos, another denominationally sponsored retirement center features townhouse-style residential areas with maintenance provided as well as laundry and housekeeping. Meals, social care, recreation and personal assistance are available as needed. A game room, chapel, library, auditorium and hospitality room are available for use by residents. Mid-rise apartments for supported living designed with special needs in mind provide the above-mentioned services with all utilities included. Transportation for shopping and medical visits is provided. For those needing nursing care, this facility provides intermediate care and longterm nursing as well as preventive services and rehabilitative therapy. Endowments and monthly fees are charged. Thirty days of health care are allotted before daily rates apply.

Carlsbad boasts a low crime rate. It offers services specifically developed for its retired populace, including a service run by a registered nurse to provide health care, home care, transportation, housekeeping and special services for retired people. Eye care, personal emergency-response systems for the elderly and a number of in-home-care programs also exist. The city has a hospice program and several intermediate-care outlets as well as an ombudsman program for elderly residents. Home weatherization and residential-shelter care are also provided for residents. There is a senior-transportation service and discounted taxi service for seniors. Volunteer programs are well-developed as are other programs sponsored by the Senior Citizens Program, 2812 San José Blvd., Carlsbad, N.M. 88220, (505) 887-7163; and Carlsbad Senior Recreation, P.O. Box 1692, Carlsbad, N.M. 88220, (505) 883-6487.

The chamber of commerce provides information about services, programs and living arrangements specifically geared toward retired persons. It sponsors a Carlsbad Area Retirement Endeavor to answer questions about

Left—*New Mexico is not only spectacular above ground, it's absolutely astounding underground, especially at Carlsbad Caverns National Park. Photo by Mark Nohl,* New Mexico Magazine.

retirement living in the community. Write to P.O. Box 910, Dept. RB, Carlsbad, N.M. 88220. You can reach the chamber at 302 S. Canal, Carlsbad, 88220; (505) 887-6516, (800) 221-1224; www.caverns.com, e-mail:chamber@caverns.com.

HOBBS—CENTER OF LEA COUNTY

Near the Texas border in the oil country of Lea County lies Hobbs (population 28,657). In 1907, a Texan named James Hobbs built his dugout house and began a school that became a social focus for local homesteaders. Soon there was a store and a post office and the fledgling town subsisted on molasses production and broom manufacturing. In 1928, Midland Co. discovered the Hobbs oil pool and the boom was on. One of the last rail lines to be built in the country was extended to Hobbs in 1913. Tent houses with corrugated iron walls sprung up. Despite Prohibition, a number of taverns vied for the roughneck trade. One tavern auctioned off a live baby alligator as a marketing ploy. When the price of oil dropped from more than a dollar to 10 cents, tin shacks were hauled away. Business has since diversified in Hobbs but the town is still dependent mainly on oil and natural gas.

The average annual temperature for the town is 62 degrees. In January, it stays in the 40s and in July it gets into the 90s. Relative humidity is from 33 percent to 66 percent, with snowfall less than 5 inches. Rain in the area is more than 14 inches and frost-free days exceed 200 per year.

Hobbs offers 13 local parks and two nearby lakes, Maddox Lake and Green Meadow just miles from town. There is a public golf course and a country club. You'll find four movie theaters in town, two skating rinks and an auto racetrack. For bowling enthusiasts, two lanes serve the community. There are three pools, 24 tennis courts and 16 ballfields. An amateur theater group presents theatrical events. New Mexico Junior College and the College of the Southwest provide educational opportunities for the community. Three libraries boast 186,000 volumes. Seven shopping centers and 10 department stores fulfill consumer needs for the community.

Commercial-air service is available three miles from town at the municipal airport. Intercity bus service is available.

Hobbs records a cost-of-living index compiled by the American Chamber of Commerce at 5 percent below the national average. Housing, utilities and miscellaneous services account for the relatively favorable costs in the town.

A new house (1,800 square feet) costs $70,894, or $38.67 a square foot. Apartments rent for $275 to $350 a month. Health care is provided by a local 250-bed hospital and a clinic. There are three nursing homes in town. The Hobbs Senior Center, P.O. Box 1117, Hobbs, N.M. 88240, provides services for the community; (505) 393-2754. AARP has an active chapter in Hobbs. Contact the Industrial Development Corp., 5625 Lovington Highway, P.O. Box 1376, Hobbs, N.M. 88240; (505) 397-2039. Contact the Hobbs Chamber of Commerce at 400 N. Marland, Hobbs, N.M. 88240; (505) 397-3202, (800) 658-6291; www.hobbschamber.org, e-mail: hobbschamber@leaco.net.

LOVINGTON—A LITTLE TOWN WITH A HEART

About 25 minutes away from Hobbs is the town of Lovington (population 9,471). Located 18 miles west of the Texas border, Lovington might seem like any other little oil patch except for one big difference—Lovington loves seniors. Mi Casa es Su Casa (my home is your home) is the name of a program specifically designed for seniors. The city and the chamber of commerce have found local retiree Ambassador Volunteers who will meet visitors at chamber headquarters and escort them around town. You can discuss your needs and plans with others who have chosen to locate in Lovington.

The town welcomes retirees and provides service and information to those who wish to locate there.

Hobbs provides connecting air service for Lovington. Intercity bus service is also available.

It is warm and pleasant in Lovington. In January, temperatures average 41 degrees; in July, around 80 degrees. There are 184 frost-free days, and humidity ranges from 30 to 52 percent. Rainfall is about 15 inches; snowfall totals around 5 inches a year.

Property taxes are moderate and so is the cost of living in Lovington. Taxes on a $65,000 brick home run a little more than $300 a year. The town promotes its low housing costs, low crime rate and a very active senior-citizen center. The 80-acre Chaparral Park is a beautiful addition to the town. It is the site of the annual World's Greatest Lizard Race.

A 28-bed acute-care facility, the Nor-Lea County Hospital, provides radiological, lab, pulmonary and physical-therapy services in addition to surgery and urological services. There are also two clinics, seven doctors and three dentists in Lovington.

The Senior Center at 115 W. Avenue O, P.O. Box 1269, Lovington, N.M. 88260, is the pride of the town; (505) 396-4161. The usual activities and services that go on in many senior centers also occur here, but the town of Lovington provides its elderly with the sense they are a real focus for the community. The chamber of commerce publishes its own senior paper and can be reached by contacting 201 S. Main, Lovington, N.M. 88260; (505) 396-5311; e-mail: visitus@leaconet.com.

ROSWELL—RETIREMENT NEW MEXICO STYLE

Roswell (population 45,293) has generated a great deal of well-earned publicity as an ideal spot to retire. In 1978, the National Municipal League chose the town as an All-American City. The 1988 *Consumer's Guide* listed Roswell as a best-rated retirement city. Hugh Bayless' book, *The Best Towns in America*, lists Roswell as a favorable place to locate. *Money* magazine says Roswell is one of the "ten towns worth calling home" and one of the "ten peaceable places to retire."

The chamber of commerce actively promotes Roswell as a retirement location. It has formed a Retirement Services Program, in which local citizens and businesses have invested. The program has produced a 25-minute video that shows all the charms and attractions of the city. It is available from the chamber for $5. You can order a copy by writing the chamber at 131 W. Second St., P.O. Drawer 70, Roswell, N.M. 88202-0070. You also can phone (505) 623-5695 or (877) 849-7679 for more information about Roswell's many attractions for retired people. Visit the town Web site at www.roswell-nm.org, e-mail: snelson@dfn.com. The chamber finances an individually tailored tour of the town that can be arranged Monday through Friday between 9 a.m. to 3 p.m. Contact the chamber to arrange weekend tours.

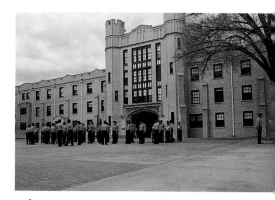

Above—*Cadets line up in formation for a general inspection at the New Mexico Military Institute (NMMI), a boarding school in Roswell for students of high school through college age. Photo by Arnold Vigil,* New Mexico Magazine.

Located in the fertile Pecos Valley, Roswell has four distinct seasons; winters are mild and summers are warm to hot. Rainfall is 14 to 16 inches a year. Precipitation falls about three to four days a month except in summer when rain occurs more frequently. In Roswell the sun shines about 75 percent of the time.

More than 19 percent of the population is retired and it is easy to see what draws people here. First, the community is conscious of the needs and desires of retired people. Second, the weather is beautiful. Third, there is still a small-town feel to the community. Fourth, there is a lot to do.

Founded in 1937, the Roswell Museum and Art Center has gained one of the finest reputations in the country. This is one example of Roswell's commitment to culture. The Community Little Theatre presents light comedies and serious dramatic productions. The Roswell Symphony performs a full season each year and also has a reputation for being one of the finest orchestras in the Southwest. Chaves County Historical Museum gives the visitor an understanding of the rich traditions of New Mexico's heritage. New Mexico Military Institute (NMMI), a highly respected military school, has the Gen.

Douglas McBride Military Museum that features exhibits of the state's military history.

A branch of Eastern New Mexico University serves every segment of the population, including the retirement-age group, with a fine schedule of courses. The city has an excellent system of 24 parks, three year-round golf courses, 30 tennis courts, a country club and the Spring River Park Zoo. Eight shopping centers make the town a regional merchandising location. Just east of Roswell, Bottomless Lakes State Park provides water sports, picnicking and fun in the sun. Bitter Lake National Wildlife Refuge protects hundreds of thousands of migratory birds and affords bird watchers unlimited opportunity to gaze at different species. Skiing and horse racing are an easy drive away at Ski Apache and Ruidoso Downs respectively.

The town has a full range of housing for rent or purchase. One-bedroom apartments rent for $150 to $450 a month and two-bedroom units or condos rent for $200 to $600. For information on HUD-subsidized apartments in Roswell, write Region VI Housing Authority, Box 2303, Roswell, N.M. 88201, or call (505) 622-0881. Depending on location and amenities, a three-bedroom house may be priced anywhere from $32,500 to $68,000. There also is a complex that styles itself as a retirement village.

Personal property tax is collected at the rate of 2.088 percent by the county. Real property tax is assessed on the basis of one-third of current appraised value at a rate of $2.47 per $100. A $65,000 home is assessed $534.71 a year.

The Roswell Police Department has 98 full-time personnel. The Chaves County sheriff's department and the state police operate outside the city. The town has 78 firemen. Water comes from pure artesian source wells that provide hard, nonflouridated water free from pollutants or bacteria.

Health-care options in Roswell have grown significantly. Roswell has the State Trauma Center. Eastern New Mexico Medical Center has 94 beds and St. Mary's Regional Health Center has 118 beds providing acute care. The latest diagnostic equipment, including CT scanners, nuclear medical equipment and angiographic facilities, is available. Coronary care, intensive care and the most modern equipment are on hand to serve the community at both facilities. The state-supported rehabilitation hospital is also in Roswell. Sixty-five physicians representing all specialty areas serve Roswell. There are 20 dentists, including specialists as well as general practitioners, nine optometrists, three opticians and seven chiropractors. An annual health fair provides free medical testing from blood pressure to diabetes for residents.

The Roswell Adult Center Courier lists more than 50 activities, events and meetings happening at the center in just a single month. There is a Senior Olympics program, Host and Hostess groups, travel presentations, dances, games, Medicare Help Program, Writer's Guild, collectors' clubs and volunteer activities. AARP and other organizations are active in Roswell. Lifelong Scholars Classes also give retirees a chance to keep learning. The center is actively supported by the city through monetary and other contributions. The Roswell Adult Center can be reached at 807 N. Missouri, Roswell, N.M. 88201; (505) 622-1450.

Three large nursing homes with more than 350 beds operate in Roswell. Two nursing homes built since 1980 feature homelike care. A number of smaller facilities can also be found in the town. One retirement inn has 109 rental suites, featuring luxury living, emergency pull cords, and a fire- and safety-alarm system. Weekly housekeeping and linen service and weekly cleaning and linen change service are provided. Planned social activities and van service are available. One- or two-bedroom apartments with a community center for group activities, a kitchen, library and game room are available at a 95-unit apartment complex in Roswell with rents from $158 for an unfurnished efficiency to $320 for a two bedroom. Monthly rentals include maintenance and utilities. Carports rent for an additional $3.50 a month. No endowment is charged.

RUIDOSO—CHARMING MOUNTAIN VILLAGE

In the northern part of the Sacramento Mountains, the mountain town of Ruidoso (elevation 6,900 feet) has much to offer the retiree. The village (population 7,698) is tucked away on the eastern slopes of the White Mountains. The climate is a delight—cool and crisp in the summer with temperatures barely reaching 80; in winter, highs are in the lower 50s. It snows in Ruidoso. And where there's snow, there's skiing. That is why the town is called the playground of the Southwest. In summer, horse racing and golf occupy the visitor.

There is a nursing home in Ruidoso, built in 1981, that has 83 beds, an

Above—*Home of the nation's richest quarter-horse race, the All American Futurity, Ruidoso Downs also offers other forms of gambling in the adjoining Billy the Kid Casino. Photo by Mark Nohl,* New Mexico Magazine.

Alzheimer's living unit with 22 beds and a developmental disability unit with 10 beds. This is the only nursing home in the vicinity and there is occasionally a waiting list, but the wait is rarely longer than two or three weeks.

The Lincoln County Health Center has full-lab facilities, an intensive-care unit, emergency room and 42 beds. There are 13 physicians, six dentists and four chiropractors in town.

The Senior Citizens Center of Lincoln County is located at 301 1/2 Junction Road, Ruidoso, N.M. 88345; (505) 257-4565. The center provides typical senior programs like shopping-escort services. The Retirement Services Division of the local chamber of commerce can inform you of all the delights of the town. Write the division at 720 Sudderth, P.O Box 698 Ruidoso, N.M. 88355; (505) 257-7395, (800) 253-2255. The chamber of commerce Web site is at www.ruidoso.net, e-mail: ruidoso@usa.net.

Near Ruidoso, the town of Lincoln is a state historic district. This is the town where Billy the Kid and Pat Garrett walked the streets. A visitor center and museum tell the story of those wild days of desperadoes and vigilantes.

SMALL-TOWN CHARM
WITH BIG-TOWN FACILITIES

Doña Ana County features one of the more well-known retirement centers in New Mexico. Las Cruces is the second largest city in the state, and the region around Las Cruces is becoming a burgeoning center for retirees. Anthony is basically a bedroom community for Las Cruces but provides a more rural, quiet, small-town atmosphere, if you find that more appealing. Hatch, "Chile Capital of the World," is not far from Las Cruces in case you're looking for an agricultural community that offers some peace and still has the advantages of close proximity to Las Cruces.

The name Doña Ana refers either to Doña Ana Robledo, an early New Mexican noble woman of legendary kindness and charity who lived in the area during the 17th century, or to an inscription on a child's grave dated in the late 1700s. Though there was some settlement here prior to the Pueblo Revolt, 1680 marks the evacuation of the area. In 1839, a grant gave land in the region to José Costales and 116 others. The town of Doña Ana lost prominence to Las Cruces in the Territorial Period. If you are interested in old buildings, Las Cruces features 100-year-old architecture, including the Amador Hotel, the Armijo House and traditional adobe houses in the Mesquite National Historic District.

Las Cruces and Anthony nestle in the

LAS CRUCES &
LOWER RIO
GRANDE VALLEY

fertile Mesilla Valley watered by the Río Grande. As one approaches from the north, the long valley opens out to breathtaking and stark vistas. The Organ Mountains provide a startling and rugged contrast to the wide valley areas, the jagged peaks breaking and rising like teeth from the flat plains below.

This is a land of vivid contrast, with desert bordering on fertile, irrigated farmlands and the mountains, ever present sentinels that provide visual relief to the openness of the landscape. The valley is becoming an increasingly popular retirement location. One can experience all four seasons, go skiing, play golf and swim in the same winter week. Las Cruces even sports a few palm trees, but the ecology and atmosphere say "high desert."

"I had my choice of retiring anywhere in the U.S.," says Raymond Kiser, who worked for many years with the U.S. Geological Survey, Water Resources Division. "I chose Las Cruces." At the end of World War II while he was in Albuquerque, Kiser headed through Las Cruces on his way to Juárez, Mexico. "I saw people standing around in their shirt sleeves on Washington's Birthday, and I thought, 'That's for me.'"

Seventeen years ago when he was in Puerto Rico on assignment, Kiser made up his mind and moved to Las Cruces. Climate had played a major role in his decision. A year in Washington, D.C., helped convince him that the warm, dry weather in Las Cruces would be a real benefit. Proximity of medical facilities and New Mexico State University as well as the abundance of activities for seniors were also factors.

"Before you move someplace, read about it and visit it," Kiser says. "Get active and go out and meet people." Kiser says a major focus for his life has been senior centers where he socializes and pursues his various interests.

ANTHONY—BEST LITTLE TOWN IN TWO STATES AND LEAP YEAR CAPITAL OF THE WORLD

There has just got to be something unpretentious and relaxed about a town that promotes itself as the "Leap Year Capital of the World." But that's Anthony.

Midway between Las Cruces (20 miles to the north) and El Paso, Texas (18 miles to the south), in the heart of the Mesilla Valley, is the town of

Above—*The fertile soil of the Mesilla Valley and the farmlands north of Las Cruces near Hatch provide ideal conditions for growing the lion's share of New Mexico's cash crops. Photo by Mark Nohl,* New Mexico Magazine.

Anthony (population 6,100 in New Mexico and 2,640 in Texas). Anthony was incorporated in Texas during 1952 and remains an unincorporated New Mexico town. This dual citizenship allows the town to participate in the destiny of both Texas and New Mexico as well as partake of the advantages of both states.

First populated by tribes such as the Mansos, Pueblos, Apaches and other Indian peoples, the region around Anthony has an abundance of Indian sites. It was a part of Mexico until late 1853 when James Gadsden, a South Carolina railroad executive, purchased territory including what was to become Anthony for a modest $10 million. The town was named after a local woman's favorite saint. It was originally called La Tuna after the prickly pear cactus indigenous to these parts. Walking excursions occur regularly into the desert to visit Indian sites and battle locations.

Early in 1988 the chamber of commerce decided to proclaim the town the "Leap Year Capital of the World" as a promotion scheme. The governors of Texas and New Mexico issued official proclamations and a New Mexico senator read the proclamation into the Congressional Record. The chamber sponsors the Worldwide Leap Year Birthday Club. Anyone born on Feb. 29 is eligible. In 1992, the town conducted a grand leap year celebration that included a Sadie Hawkins Day carnival, golf tournament and a giant birthday cake. For those looking to relocate in a small town near the larger retirement market of Las Cruces and close to urban El Paso and the Mexican border, Anthony offers distinct advantages. The Río Grande winds through the Mesilla Valley on its way to the Gulf of Mexico. The river has created a fertile lush area, turning the Anthony region into a Garden of Eden from spring to fall. Cotton, chile, lettuce, onions, pecans, apples and wine grapes are grown here.

Above—Colorful Mexican-folklorico dancers kick up their heels to the vibrating sounds of mariachi music in front of the gazebo on the Plaza during a fiesta in Old Mesilla. Photo by Pamela Porter.

At 3,881 feet, Anthony's annual temperature is 85 degrees. In January the average temperature is 58 degrees; in July it is 93 degrees. Annual rainfall is about 8 inches, with winds prevailing from the southwest. The Organ and Franklin mountains protect Anthony and surrounding regions from severe weather and offer residents incredible opportunities to witness glorious sunrises and sunsets.

The largest employer in town is Mountain Pass Canning Co., which cans chile and provides work to more than 700 Anthony residents. Anthony also serves as a bedroom community to professionals who commute to White Sands Missile Range, Fort Bliss, Holloman Air Force Base, New Mexico State University (NMSU) and the University of Texas at El Paso (UTEP). The proximity of the two universities offer residents many educational opportunities. Emphasis at NMSU is on research and there are strong ties to NASA programs at White Sands.

Anthony is served by three local fire departments and law-enforcement agencies from both Texas and New Mexico.

There are two golf courses—the private Anthony Country Club and Dos Lagos Club—and 63 acres of public parks and recreational areas with several baseball fields. Four tennis courts and one swimming pool serve the town. The Río Grande offers Anthony residents year-round outdoor recreation, with a focus on fishing. Mountains to the north and west provide skiing in the winter and hiking in the summer within a few hours of town. To the north, Caballo and Elephant Butte reservoirs offer boating and water recreation. White Sands National Monument museum and playground also are close at hand. Minutes away, the Santa Teresa Country Club has two 18-hole golf courses and Sunland Park racetrack provides horse-racing excitement for residents.

Las Cruces and El Paso are only about a half-hour away and offer all the opportunities of larger metropolitan areas. Mexico is just to the south for those who wish to sample another culture, outdoor *mercados* (markets) and the history and romance of our international neighbor to the south. The chamber of commerce can direct you to a number of motor-touring opportunities all within easy driving distance of town.

Anthony is oriented to single-family housing. There are many good buying opportunities. On the New Mexico side, home prices start about $5,000 less than on the Texas side. The resale home market runs from about $25,000 to $35,000. Near Dos Lagos Golf Course homes are priced from $55,000 to $95,000. Anthony Country Club also offers luxury living only minutes from town. In town, lots go for $5,000 to $7,000. Prime development areas are priced at about $10,500 an acre. Rural housing is hard to find. Prices start at $85,000, but views of the mountains and valleys are well worth it.

Anthony features one retirement facility, a 32-unit apartment complex that qualifies for HUD support. Several organizations in town are of interest for seniors. The VFW has a local chapter and the American Legion is active. The town has a Senior Center that provides meal services through Services for Seniors Inc. Home meals are also available. For more information contact Anthony Community Improvement Association, P.O. Box 518, Anthony, N.M. 88021.

A chiropractor, three doctors, two medical clinics, two pharmacies and one local dental clinic serve Anthony. The town has its own branch of the New Mexico Department of Health and two full-service ambulance facilities. Las Cruces offers one major hospital and El Paso has one military hospital and 12 civilian hospitals.

For further information, call the Anthony Chamber of Commerce at (505) 882-5677 or write P.O. Box 1086, Anthony, N.M. 88021.

HATCH—CHILE CAPITAL OF THE WORLD

Hatch (population 1,673) is an agricultural center nestled in the heart of the Hatch Valley. It boasts one of the finest chile harvests in the world. For two days over the Labor Day weekend, the air fills with the scent of chile as the local chile queen rules over the colorful and spicy Chile Festival.

The climate is mild, with temperatures averaging 79.1 degrees. Precipitation is only 8.96 inches a year. White Sands Missile Range employs many of its 1,084 citizens. Hatch's location just south of Caballo Reservoir and 36 miles north of Las Cruces is causing retirees to sit up and take notice of the village.

The Hatch Senior Center is just adjacent to the local library and museum, P.O. Box 404, Hatch, N.M. 87937; (505) 267-4813. The Ben Archer Health Clinic provides medical and dental services. There is a 268-bed county hospital available, four nursing homes and two retirement homes located nearby. The Valley Chamber of Commerce can be reached at P.O. Box 38, Hatch, N.M. 87937; (505) 267-5050.

LAS CRUCES—PRIME RETIREMENT DESTINATION

A lot has changed in Las Cruces since the wild Southwest days when Pat Garrett, legendary hero who shot Billy the Kid, was himself mysteriously murdered.

Now the second largest town in New Mexico, Las Cruces (population 74,267) is a prime retirement destination. According to Rand McNally, Las Cruces ranks among the top communities in the Southwest for retirement, ahead of Tucson and right behind Phoenix. The general population in Las Cruces grew almost 23 percent from 1980 to 1985, or 2.9 percent per annum. This ranked the southern New Mexico community among the top-20, fastest-growing communities in the country. Between the beginning of the decade and 1987, Las Cruces' growth rate for people older than 63 has been 9 to 10 percent per year.

There are many reasons why Las Cruces (elevation 3,896 feet) continues to attract retirement-age residents. Bordered by the jagged peaks of the Organ Mountains to the east and the fabled Río Grande to the west, Las Cruces has wonderful climatic conditions.

The annual average temperature is a little more than 60 degrees. In January, the average temperature is 41.6 degrees; in July, 79.5 degrees. The

Right—A yucca plant, New Mexico's state flower, decorates the desert floor in front of the Organ Mountains at Aguirre Springs National Recreation Site east of Las Cruces. Photo by Mark Nohl, New Mexico Magazine.

average frost-free period is from April to the end of October. Temperatures of zero or below have occurred only eight days in the 85 years temperatures have been recorded. Snow seldom stays on the ground more than two days. The sun shines 350 days a year, with average relative afternoon humidity a pleasant 27 percent. Rainfall is 8.49 inches and snowfall is 3.3 inches a year.

In addition to the climate, quality of life is very high, offering advantages of a small city without the drawbacks of large, urban areas. The town is only an hour away from the markets, color and culture of Juárez, Mexico. Las Cruces itself has retained a Southwest flavor. Remains of some of the oldest structures in the country have been found in the Mesilla Valley, remains that record the presence of Pueblo peoples who lived in the area from A.D. 300 to 1450, when they vanished. The area is rich in early Spanish history. Alvar Núñez Cabeza de Vaca made his way into the valley in 1535. Oñate later led hundreds of settlers along El Camino Real (King's Highway) past what was to become Las Cruces. The town is named for an event that occurred in 1830 when a caravan from Taos was ambushed by Apaches. When the dead were buried and their graves were marked with crosses, the location became known as La Placita de las Cruces (place of the crosses)—Las Cruces for short.

The village of La Mesilla near Las Cruces preserves the flavor of these early days with its thick adobe walls that protected residents against Apache attacks.

Now visitors stroll from art galleries to museums and gift shops.

Located at the crossroads of the old Camino Real and the Butterfield Overland stage route, this New Mexico village dates from the late 1500s. The village retains the charm and ambiance of bygone days and has art galleries and small shops. Here on the Plaza in 1854 the U.S. flag was raised, confirming the Gadsden Purchase and officially reorganizing this portion of southern New Mexico as part of the United States. It is here that Billy the Kid escaped from jail after being sentenced for murder.

Above—*The historic streets of the Old Mesilla Plaza simultaneously exude the charm of Colonial New Mexico and the flavor of Old Mexico. Photo by Mark Nohl,* New Mexico Magazine.

The Las Cruces area boasts exceptional agricultural produce. Fields of cotton, pecan groves, vineyards and chile now stand on land that was once inhospitable desert. Local growers offer their produce at the Farmer's Market each Wednesday and Saturday morning on the Downtown Mall.

Because of the mild climate in Las Cruces, outdoor sports are enjoyed year-round. Four golf courses operate in town. Tennis is played at 14 city courts. There also is horseback riding along the Río Grande, fishing in the Gila Wilderness area or to the north at Elephant Butte Reservoir, and hiking at Aguirre Springs National Recreation Site and in the Organ Mountains. Sunland Park, 40 miles south of Las Cruces, has horse racing from October through May. For the more sedentary, Las Cruces also has two libraries and two museums.

Interstates provide service east and west as well as north and south. El Paso International Airport is 50 minutes from Las Cruces by car, and AMTRAK also serves El Paso. Las Cruces has intercity bus service as well as a city bus system and commercial-air service at the municipal airport.

Cloudcroft and Ruidoso ski areas are within a couple of hours from Las Cruces. There are 58 parks in Las Cruces, six swimming pools, a skating rink,

15 handball courts, a bowling alley and three performing-arts theaters. New Mexico State University is the cultural center for the town. Major classical, jazz and popular music concerts are regularly featured on campus. The Las Cruces Symphony hosts many guest artists, and the American Southwest Theatre Company with the affiliation of nationally known playwright Mark Medoff offers a full season of productions.

Annual events fill the Las Cruces calendar. In early September, the Whole Enchilada Hot-Air Balloon Rally sets the sky ablaze with color and excitement. The Southern New Mexico State Fair later that month features exhibits and mid-way entertainment. The Sheriff's Posse Rodeo brings the old Southwest alive during the fall. In early October, the Whole Enchilada Fiesta celebrates for three days with parades, entertainment, sporting events and arts and crafts, climaxed by cooking and serving the world's largest enchilada. In November the Renaissance Craftfaire occurs in Young Park. The convention and visitor's bureau can tell you more about the full schedule of events. Write 211 N. Water St., Las Cruces, N.M. 88001; (505) 541-2444, (800) 343-7827; www.lascrucescvb.org, e-mail: cvb@lascruces.org.

Las Cruces has become increasingly attentive to retirement-age people, who are an important segment of the local population. The median price for an existing three-bedroom home is about $102,500. For a new three-bedroom home the median price is around $141,000. Condos and townhomes also are for sale. The local chamber of commerce offers prospective residents a handy list of mobile home parks, campgrounds, apartments and real estate agents available in Las Cruces. Property tax rates in the area are relatively low.

Health services in Las Cruces are among the finest in the state. Memorial General Hospital is a 286-bed, acute-care facility that staffs 108 staff physicians in 24 different specialties. The radiology unit has a body CT scanner. There are nuclear medicine, mammography, ultrasound, gastroenterology, echocardiology, renal-dialysis, dietetics, chemotherapy, pulmonary-function and therapy services. A cancer-treatment center also has been completed within walking distance of the main hospital. Las Cruces also has five smaller hospitals (two psychiatric) with a total of 197 beds, seven clinics, 136 physicians and 41 dentists. The town has four nursing homes totaling 193 beds and two retirement homes offering 139 beds. William Beaumont Military Hospital is located in El Paso for veterans seeking medical treatment.

One retirement village offers residents 159 apartments and a 60-unit, health-care center affiliated with a major Protestant denomination. There are nine apartment styles ranging from studio to two bedroom with a choice of one or two baths. Monthly service fees provide apartment maintenance, ground services, security, lounge and recreation areas, swimming pool, Jacuzzi and gardens. There is an entrance fee that is half-refundable upon sale or vacancy. Add-ons are charged for living on second and third floors. There is also an additional charge if an extra person occupies with the main tenant. Meals are charged extra per month. Five day's non-cumulative yearly health care is provided for residents. The health-care center is on call day or night with call buttons furnished in apartments. There is also a hospital across the street from the village. Monthly maid service, coin-operated laundries on each floor, barber and beauty shop, paid utilities, dining room, transportation service, planned social and recreational activities, a full activities center and library are some of the amenities.

In addition, Las Cruces has five smaller nursing homes, ranging from a very small guesthouse to a health-care center. Munson Senior Center is a multi-purpose 19,500-square-foot senior center with a dining area, meeting room and ballroom, arts and crafts rooms, library and quiet rooms, classrooms and offices for home care, senior companions, transportation and other services. Voluntary membership fees are $5.

A full range of arts and crafts activities occur at the center, including painting, drawing, calligraphy, knitting, needlepoint, leather work, lapidary and stained glass. Recreational activities include slimnastics and aerobics, cards, puzzles and games, chair exercise, folk dancing, square dancing, pool, chorus, pingpong and shuffleboard. Classes also go on at the center, including programs in English, Spanish, creative writing, Bible study, health education, crime prevention and a lecture series.

Home care and transportation, blood-pressure clinics, cancer screening, a noon-meal program, tax assistance and outreach are among the services the center provides.

Noon meals are furnished to those 60 years and older and a modest $3 charge is assessed those under 60. Information about activities, programs and classes can be obtained by writing the center at 975 S. Mesquite, P.O. Drawer CLC, Las Cruces, N.M. 88004; (505) 526-2492.

Above—*The fruits and labor of southern New Mexico's fertile valleys are quite evident at the farmer's market during the annual Whole Enchilada Festival in Las Cruces. Photo by Mark Nohl,* New Mexico Magazine.

Mesilla Park Senior Center also provides services and meals. The center is open from 8 a.m. to 1 p.m., Monday through Friday. Monday and Wednesday crafts classes, exercise classes with blood-pressure checks once a month and ceramic classes on Tuesday and Thursday comprise some of the offerings at the center. The Mesilla Center can be contacted at 304 W. Bell, Mesilla Park, N.M. 88047; (505) 524-2657. Services for Seniors Inc. also operates in east Las Cruces. The company provides home-delivered meals for housebound seniors 60 years or older. This organization has 12 distribution centers in the county. Homemaker and transportation services are also provided. Also, for information on Retired Senior Volunteer Programs in the Las Cruces area, write Aurora Ybarra, Director RSVP, City of Las Cruces, P.O. Drawer CLC, Las Cruces, N.M. 88004; (505) 526-0604.

Further information of interest to retirees can be obtained from the Las Cruces Chamber of Commerce, 760 W. Picacho, P.O. Drawer 519, Las Cruces, N.M. 88004; (505) 524-1968; www.lascruces.org, e-mail: chamber@huntleigh.net.